Women at
the Beginning

Women at
the Beginning

*Origin Myths
from the Amazons
to the Virgin Mary*

PATRICK J. GEARY

Princeton University Press
PRINCETON AND OXFORD

Copyright © 2006 by Princeton University Press
Published by Princeton University Press, 41 William Street,
Princeton, New Jersey 08540
In the United Kingdom: Princeton University Press,
3 Market Place, Woodstock, Oxfordshire OX20 1SY

Library of Congress Cataloging-in-Publication Data
Geary, Patrick J., 1948–
Women at the beginning : origin myths from the Amazons
to the Virgin Mary / Patrick J. Geary.
p. cm.
Includes bibliographical references (p.) and index.
ISBN-13: 978-0-691-12409-4 (cl : alk. paper)
ISBN-10: 0-691-12409-4 (cl : alk. paper)
1. Women—Mythology. 2. Beginning—Mythology. I. Title.
BL795.W65G43   2006
201′.3′082—dc22   2005047630

British Library Cataloging-in-Publication Data is available

This book has been composed in Minion

Printed on acid-free paper. ∞

pup.princeton.edu

Printed in the United States of America

10 9 8 7 6 5 4 3 2 1

For Mary

at the beginning
and forever

Contents

Acknowledgments

Lawrence Stone changed my life in the autumn of 1972 by inviting me to interview for a position at Princeton University. While my training in the Medieval Studies Program at Yale University under the direction of Robert Lopez and Jaroslav Pelikan taught me to be a medievalist, my years on the Princeton faculty and in particular participating in the weekly meetings of the Shelby Cullom Davis Center seminars, presided over by Stone, taught me most of what I know about being a historian. Thus it was a particular pleasure to have been invited by Anthony Grafton and William Jordan as the Lawrence Stone Visiting Professor at Princeton University in 2002. While researching a previous book that dealt with the relationship between contemporary nationalism and medieval origin myths, I had been fascinated by the place that women held (or did not hold) in these myths.[1] The series of lectures I gave at Princeton that year provided me the opportunity to return to these texts with a different set of questions, questions about the representation of women in the origins of families, peoples, nations, and religions.

While at Princeton in 2002, Anthony Grafton, William Jordan, Adelaide Bennet, and Peter Brown helped me recognize some of the fundamental issues at stake in this project. In Europe, Herwig Wolfram and Walter Pohl, who have pioneered the study not only of early medieval origin myths but of the gender implications of these complex traditions, generously shared their work in progress on the topic. Dušan Třeštík and Petra Mutlova have kindly assisted me with the Czech tradition. Megan Cassidy-Welch and her colleagues in Melbourne and Margaret Clunies Ross in Sydney helped me think through these issues in the context of Australian medieval studies. At UCLA, Anver Emon and Boris Todorov have educated me on texts and issues in, respectively, Islam and Eastern Europe, while Christopher Baswell has shared with me his work on gender and origins in the later Middle Ages. Lisa Bitel and Janet L. Nelson have been particularly helpful in guiding me in the literature of feminist and gender studies, and Elizabeth Parker McLachlan shared her knowledge of the iconographic tradition of the Jesse Tree. Karl Brunner read and commented on a first draft of the manuscript, and Blair Sullivan and Holly Grieco worked diligently to assist me in the final preparation of the book. I am grateful to Beth Gianfagna for her careful editorial work.

An earlier version of parts of chapter 2 appeared in *Die Suche nach den Ursprüngen,* edited by Walter Pohl.[2]

Women at
the Beginning

Introduction

So when the woman saw that the tree was good for food, and that it was a delight to the eyes, and that the tree was to be desired to make one wise, she took of its fruit and ate; and she also gave some to her husband, and he ate.[1]

[Heracles] found in a cave a creature of double form that was half damsel and half serpent; above the buttocks she was a woman, below them a snake.[2]

After [Tanausis's] death, while the army under his successors was engaged in an expedition in other parts, a neighboring tribe attempted to carry off women of the Goths as booty. But they made a brave resistance, as they had been taught to do by their husbands, and routed in disgrace the enemy who had come upon them. When they had won this victory, they were inspired with greater daring. Mutually encouraging each other, they took up arms and chose two of the bolder, Lampeto and Marpesia, to act as their leaders.[3]

Then Gambara went to Frea, the wife of Wodan, and asked that the victory go to the Winili. Frea gave the advice that the women of the Winili should let down their hair and tie it around their faces in the manner of a beard and they should gather at dawn with their men in that place where they would be seen by Wodan when, as was his wont, he looked through the eastern window. They did this. When Wodan looked east he said, "Who are these Longibardi?" Then Frea added that he should give the victory to those to whom he had given a name."[4]

The youngest daughter, Libuše, was the most marvelous of the three . . . : wise in council, powerful in speech, chaste in body, outstanding in morals, second to none in her concern for justice, affable to all, a glory and decoration of the female sex . . . . But, since no one is in every way good, this praiseworthy woman—oh sad human estate—was a seer.[5]

. . . which most prudent and beautiful Judith the most powerful Count Baldwin joined to himself in matrimony. From her he engendered a son, giving him his own name, that is Baldwin.[6]

Heli begat Joseph; Joseph begat Joachim; Joachim begat Mother Mary, Mother of the Lord Jesus Christ.[7]

These texts, which span over a thousand years of time and an equally great spectrum of cultures and traditions, have in common that their authors, all men, are in some way writing about the beginnings: the beginnings of peoples, of families, of nations, of religions. They also share in common a need to fix the place of women in these beginnings. On the one hand, from the earliest accounts of peoples in Herodotus, to the genealogies in sacred scripture and later religious traditions, to legends of the founding of ancient cities, to early medieval accounts of the peoples who displaced Roman political authority in the West, to noble families' genealogies constructed in the eleventh century and beyond, women, while present, play usually at best a marginal role. Some are but names; wombs that make possible the transmission of male virtue from generation to generation. Prominent women are often distinguished by their wickedness. Women such as Dido and Eve, some medieval Islamic versions of Sarah,[8] the Frankish princess Amalberga in the Saxon origin story told by Widukind of Corvey[9] or Rosamund in the story of the Lombard hero Alboin,[10] are the source of sin and conflict. But there are other, more complex women: magical women such as Gambara, mother of the first Lombard dukes, and Libuše, Kazi, and Tetka, the three magical sisters in Cosmas of Prague's account of the origins of the Czechs;[11] women such as Lilith who engender races of monsters by consorting with demons[12] and the Gothic witches from whom sprang the Huns;[13] saintly women like Clothild, wife of the Frankish king Clovis[14] or Dobrava, wife of the Polish Duke Mieszko[15] who were responsible for converting their husbands and thus their peoples in the tradition of St. Helen.[16] There were monstrous women like the mother of the Scyths in Herodotus or Melusine, foundress of the Lusignan family's prosperity, who were part serpent and part human.[17] And there was Mary—in one Jewish tradition a fallen woman who foisted off her bastard child by a Roman soldier on her gullible husband, in Islam "above the women of all created beings," and in Christianity the Mother of all faithful.

The men who wrote about these women often held ambivalent attitudes toward them, attitudes that are evident in the contradictory images produced and reproduced across the centuries. As the French historian Jean-Claude Schmitt has written concerning the powerful but ambivalent images of Eve and Pandora, when studying these accounts the historian must understand the different meanings that they held for the societies that produced them, taking into account in particular the variants chosen or invented in the course of their reception.[18] The representations of women in stories of beginnings, as Amazons or saints, monsters or troublemakers, are too complex to categorize. They remain problematic and contradictory figures. And yet they continue to fascinate, to tempt us to consider them, to ask what the place of women at the beginning tells us about women, about beginnings, and about the present and future.

The chapters that follow, originally given as lectures, first at Princeton University and then, in various versions at a number of other institutions, explore specific cases from this vast panorama of the European tradition from antiquity until the twelfth century of women at the beginning. While not intended as a comprehensive examination of women in origin legends, they suggest that writing about women at the beginning could be a means by which authors tried to come to terms with their ambivalences about women in their own worlds.

This ambivalence was much weaker in antiquity than in the Christian Middle Ages. Within the Greco-Roman tradition, women's places in origin stories were marginal, when indeed they were present at all. Whatever may have been the complex roles of women in classical societies, women in the origin accounts that have come to us were firmly in the control of masculine ideological agendas. If present, women at the beginning tended to die violently so that proper, male civilization could develop. The complexities of late antiquity and the early Middle Ages complicated this situation considerably, both because of the ambiguous and paradoxical tradition of Christianity vis à vis Mary and because of the complexities of reproducing and transmitting power and authority in medieval society.

Rather than attempting a coherent narrative creating some putative linear development of women in origin myths from antiquity to the High Middle Ages, I have chosen to take specific moments and specific texts that illuminate key aspects of this complex problem, to look at how authors struggle with received traditions, cultural norms, and their own experiences to make sense of the contradictions and revelations in prototypical stories of women, origins, and power. From the Amazons to the Virgin Mary, from magical prophetesses to Frankish noblewomen, we see some of the same issues, crossing boundaries, informing different registers of discourse, and producing, with powerful and creative tensions and contradictions, the complexities of a European tradition.

The chapters that follow examine different moments and clusters of texts but nevertheless explore a common theme: the tensions between ideological programs and lived experience. This approach attempts to engage some of the basic and ongoing debates in gender history as developed particularly among medievalists in the past decades. On the one hand, scholars such as Georges Duby, examining representations of women in some of these very texts, read them as evidence that women became progressively silent, marginalized in society, and virtually irretrievable to history.[19] This reading of medieval women has been massively rejected by most historians who study women in the Middle Ages. Instead, more recent scholarship has pointed out not only the continuing prominence of women of power in public life in the twelfth century and beyond but also of the necessity to revise assumptions about structural changes such as the rise of primogeniture in Europe's aristocracy and the transformation of the kindred from horizontal, bilateral kin groups to narrow, vertical lineages.[20] But if this is so, what then is to be made of the literature explored by Duby? The essays that follow attempt to answer this question by suggesting that the literary texts that attempt to eliminate or circumscribe the place of women as foundational and thus as exemplary figures in constructed narratives of origins are less a reflection of women's lack of power than a reflection of the paradoxes of masculine ideologies that are forced to contend with the massive contradictions of lived experience. Unable to eliminate women from the practice of public power, perhaps even unwilling to do so, these clerical authors eliminate them from the only world over which they have full control: the world of texts.

Women and Origins in Antiquity and the Early Middle Ages

Why concentrate on women at the beginning if what we want to understand is rather the development of mental horizons across centuries of the Middle Ages? What is it about beginnings that draws us? Do beginnings contain an embryo of that which is to come, some essential DNA of the future of a society, a movement, or a people that determines forever its ultimate meaning?

Idols and Idolaters

Marc Bloch, the great twentieth-century historian, resistance fighter, and martyr, dedicated a section of his unfinished essay, *Apologie pour l'histoire*, or *The Historian's Craft*, to what he called "The Idol of Origins."[1] He observes that historians, himself included, have a tendency to prioritize both the most recent and the most distant pasts to the point of hypnotism. He goes on to ask what exactly one means by origins and what the obsession with origins on the part of historians is actually all about. If one meant simply the start, such an interest would be acceptable, although he warns that the start of things is always extremely difficult to determine, and thus such investigations are generally futile. However, he suggests, when historians ask about origins we really mean causes, specifically causes that explain; and what is worse, all too often we are searching for causes that explain everything. "There," he says, "lies the ambiguity, and there the danger!"[2]

We do well to recognize this danger at the beginning of an investigation into women at the origin: at the origin of families, of nations, of religions, of peoples. By asking about how women are represented in the foundation legends of social phenomena, are we seeking something timeless, essential, and explanatory, either about human societies in general or about the particular cultures that created them? Are we examining something essential about the very nature of gender constructions in human society? Or are we looking for a key to understanding the actual place of women in the formation and coherence of these cultures? There are serious people who would answer a resounding yes to all of these questions. For some, legends of women at the beginning form a pentimento, an overpainted but still dimly perceptible recollection of an age of matriarchy.[3] For such scholars, the study of women at the beginning is just what it says it is: an examination into the condition of women who gave birth to social forms only to find themselves and their daughters suppressed, marginalized, and silenced by their male offspring.[4]

For others, the study of women at the beginning is an attempt to discover, within genealogies, origin legends, and chronicles, the lived reality of women at the earliest periods of specific social and cultural constellations. Do such texts actually reflect social roles and options in emerging communities? Should the persistent accounts of Amazons among barbarian peoples in antiquity and the early Middle Ages, for example, be taken seriously as evidence that women fought alongside their men in these societies?

This is by no means an unreasonable suggestion. As we shall see in greater detail in chapter 2, Amazons figure prominently not only in classical ethnographic accounts and origin legends from the time of Herodotus through the Middle Ages but also in Roman and medieval accounts of campaigns against "barbarian" Celts, Germanic enemies, and Steppe peoples.[5] Moreover, archaeological evidence of women buried with weapons occurs in ancient and medieval tombs from the area of the Black Sea.[6] In light of such evidence, perhaps descriptions of Amazons are simply reflections of reality.

One can ask similar questions about the magical women who appear in other origin legends. If Libuše, the legendary mother of the Czech people, is described as a *phitonissa*, a seer, and if we hear that a phitonissa accompanied a Polish army as late as 1209,[7] ought we to conclude that the twelfth-century chronicle of Cosmas of Prague provides us with an accurate insight into the early role of women as prognosticators in west Slavic societies?

These questions are legitimate, and yet they risk, I believe, the dangers enunciated by Marc Bloch. Such a search for "women at the beginning" all too easily can become not so much a search for the start as an essentialized search for the root causes of gender divisions, patriarchy, and societal forms. All too often such investigations, unconsciously or not, posit what was at the beginning as what was right, and understand the contrast between these projected images of founding women and subsequent gender roles as a falling away, a perversion, or a loss. Whether or not such judgments are valid, they are not historical judgments.

Thus I will pursue neither the big questions of what origin legends can tell us about prepatriarchal societies nor whether they can actually tell us about the original gender boundaries of these societies. I will not look for the "facts" in depictions of women as saints or monsters, clairvoyants or warriors. However, this does not mean that in what follows I am not interested in the Idol of Origins. In fact, this is exactly my prey, but in a different way: I pursue not the idol but the idolaters.

The compilers, authors, genealogists, theologians, and lawyers who compiled these origin myths were for the most part engaged in exactly what Bloch warns against: these authors are never interested in the search for origins as a search for the start. Their goal is always the present and future: their investigations are precisely intended to explain—to explain causes, to explain essences, to explain how the world was and how it should be. For these authors, the origins of a people, a family, a nation, does indeed hold great meaning for the present and future; the model of generation, of descent, whether physical or moral, is essential not only for identity but for value. As the German scholar Gerd Melville suggests, "The period that reaches from the origins to the present must be presented as an uninterrupted series of concrete acts that honor primordial qualities."[8] And yet, these explorations of origins are in constant tension between their sources and their contemporary milieus. But here lies a basic problem: their sources, whether oral or written, indigenous or classical, derive from worlds very different from the author's own, presenting values, behavior, and patterns at odds with what, from the perspective of these authors, ought to be. And yet hallowed as sacred scripture, as classics of Greco-Roman culture, or venerable tradition, these traditions could not be simply rejected or suppressed: somehow they had to be given contemporary meaning. The result is paradox, a tension, between incomprehensible tradition and the urgency for meaning.

And nowhere is the paradox greater than in the place of women in these origins, because this meaning involves, explicitly or implicitly, gendered power relations that these authors experience in their own worlds.

The Classical Heritage

Medieval textual culture depends enormously on the twin heritages of classical and biblical antiquity. Medievals were never slavish in their uses of either, no matter how adamantly they pretended to be so. Nevertheless, models, themes, and possibilities of describing the human condition, including human origins, derive in large part from this inheritance. And yet the distance between classical gender assumptions and those of even learned medieval authors is vast. The differences can only be appreciated if we begin with antiquity, when beginnings were clearly an affair of men.

Beginnings should begin with men. From the fifth century B.C.E., as western Eurasian societies thought about the continuities between the past and the present, their intellectuals, almost exclusively men, understood these continuities as generations of men. They are the appropriate subject of history; they provide the continuity in genealogy; they give order and meaning across time. As the *Glossa ordinaria*, echoing St. Ambrose and others put it, "Non est consuetudo Scripturarum, ut ordo mulierum in generationibus texatur" (It is not the custom of the sacred scriptures that the order of women would be woven into generations).[9] Organizing the past in terms of generations was the fundamental mode of historical thinking. As the American philologist R. Howard Bloch suggests, "From the fourth century on, the defining mode of universal history was that of genealogy," and fathers were "the prime subject of historical enunciation and children its object."[10] Bloch was writing about the fourth century C.E., but his comments are just as applicable to antiquity as well. But in such a conception of history, one must ask what then were mothers, either historically or grammatically?

Certainly, prior to the brave new world of cloning, reproduction, biological or cultural, demanded not only men but women. And just as certainly, authors assiduously tracing the grammar of universal history were well aware of women exercising great authority not only in the distant past but in their own times. Writing about women, power, and generation at the beginning became a way of writing about women, power, and generation in the present. If the complexities of women's roles in generation, legitimization, and power could not be resolved, at least exemplary accounts could be means of expressing the paradoxes of the problem and perhaps of resolving in the past what could not be resolved in the present.

Women and Power in Classical Antiquity

Classical ethnography is essential for the understanding of the long history of women's place in European origin legends, and this tradition starts with Herodotus.[11] His reports on the origins of the Scyths provide fundamental models of origin traditions, both in general and in the way that he uses the females in the Greek version of the Scythian origin to marginalize this society, that were repeated by later Greek, Roman, and Byzantine chroniclers, and ultimately transmitted indirectly to Western medieval authors. Herodotus offers three versions of the Scythian ethnogenesis. The first and most famous account is what he describes as the Scyths' own story, which begins with one Targitaus, said to be the son of Zeus and an unnamed daughter of the River Dorysthenes (the Dnieper). They produced three sons, Lipoxaïs, Arpoxaïs, and Colaxaïs, each of whom is credited with being the father of a Scythian *genus*, although the youngest, Colaxaïs, alone received divine approval to be made king.[12] In this version, nothing is said about the female river spirit—the emphasis of the story is elsewhere and may well reflect an internal understanding of Scythian self-identity, tied to an agricultural rather than pastoral society, although apparently misunderstood or misrepresented by Herodotus.

The account of the origins of the Scyths that Herodotus attributed to the Pontic Greeks is much more concerned with the mother of the Scyths, but a mother who embodies their marginalization from the human race. We hear that Heracles came into the country now called Scythia, driving the cattle he had obtained from Geryon, and fell asleep. While he slept, his mares, that had been yoked to his chariot, disappeared. Searching for them he found in a cave a creature of double form, half woman and half serpent. She told Heracles that she had his mares but would not return them unless he had intercourse with her. This he did. The result was three sons, Agathyrsus, Gelonus, and Scythes, the youngest, who alone passed a test of strength and became the father of the Scyths.

The third account, which Herodotus prefers, actually is not an origin story at all but explains that nomadic Scythians migrated from Asia, defeated the Cimmerians, and took over their territory.

The essential elements of these three accounts (origins of a people described in terms of the origin of a family or an account of migration, assuming a previous origin; divine sanction; ancestry from Heracles; ancestry from a women who is either part divine or part monster) recur and resonate throughout classical and medieval ethnography. The second origin myth, the birth of the Scyths from a *mixoparthenos*, is, however, especially significant for our inquiry.

The mixoparthenos, the snake woman of the Pontic Greeks' origin account, is particularly interesting because it is, as the French classicist François Hartog has argued, a way for Greeks to "think nomadism," that is, to conceive of an origin appropriate to a people who are, if not in their own minds, at least in the minds of the Greeks, the archetypical nomads.[13] Heracles is the father of many cities and barbarian peoples.[14] In this particular origin story, he is father of a people at the extreme ends of the world. Herodotus tells us that he arrived in Scythia from

Geryon, who lived outside the Pontus at the edge of the world. The geographic marginality of the Scyths is paralleled by their marginal relationship to the human race. Their mother is only part human: she belongs to the same order of half-human, half-serpent creatures as Echidna, who in Hesiod's *Theogony*, is born of Phorkys and Keto. Echidna too has offspring, but they are themselves monsters: Orthus (the dog of Geryon), Cerberus, the Hydra of Lerna, and the Chimera, the Sphinx, and the Nemean Lion. The Scyths are, like these monsters, utterly different from the Greeks, that is, from full humanity.

The key to understanding this account is to remember that it is a Greek, not a Scythian, version of Scythian origins. The Scythian origin legend, to the extent that Herodotus can be credited with reporting it with some accuracy, assigns the maternal role to a river deity, even if her story is not particularly developed in the account. For Greeks, mothers fit poorly into accounts of origins, and motherhood becomes essentially negative: the means by which the Scyths are doubly marginalized from the Greeks, not only by their geographical location on the edge of the world but by their descent from a snake woman.

At least the Scyths had a mother. From an Athenian perspective, this could be understood more as a defect than a virtue. Of all Western societies, Periclean Athens came closest to eliminating altogether women at the beginning, to achieve what J.-P. Vernant terms the Greek male's ideal, the "dream of a purely paternal descendant."[15] Athenians are autochthons: In the Athenian origin myth, the first male springs from the earth. In a variant, Erichtonios is produced when Hephaistos, lusting after Athena, chases her and ejaculates onto her leg. She wipes off the sperm with a bit of wool, throws it on the earth. The earth is impregnated and produces a male child. Athena then lifts him from the earth and sees to his education.[16] Women, in contrast, are the work of artisans: Pandora, the first woman, was made, not born, thus denying the existence of a first Athenian woman or indeed any Athenian woman.[17] The problems of this extreme elimination of women from the beginning were, however, enormous: at the same time that Athenian ideology denied women identity as Athenians, the law of 451/50 required that a citizen be born of a father and mother who were both citizens. The result was an insoluble paradox.

Roman accounts do not deny female origin legends, but these tend to be negative or sacrificial. The most significant is that of Carthage, the city founded by Dido. Antiquity knew various versions of Dido, just as it knew various versions of the origins of the Scyths and other peoples. While in both traditions Dido flees Tyre after her brother murders her husband, founds Carthage, and initiates its rise, the two accounts diverge greatly in recounting her fate. In one version, Dido is an excellent queen who only kills herself because, as an exemplary widow, she rejects the demands of her followers to marry a local prince. In the other, which derives largely from Virgil, she commits suicide out of mad and hopeless love for Aeneas, who has abandoned her.[18] In Virgil's account, in the words of Christopher Baswell, the "dominant version of the myth (the *Aeneid*), produced for a dominant class," Dido's intelligence and shrewdness are suppressed as part of a systematic suppression of Dido as model of clever, mercantile and specifically feminine power.[19] Not only does she change into a mad, sex-crazed suicide from a chaste widow who prefers death to a forced marriage, but her cleverness and ingenuity in the foundation of Carthage disappears as well. The alternative Dido survived in a shadowy existence, in accounts by minor historians and Virgilian commentators, to emerge only at the end of antiquity, and she would not receive a major voice until the Middle Ages.[20]

Women in the various accounts of Rome's own origins suffer a similar fate. The most fortunate, one might say, is Lavinia, the daughter of Latinus and promised bride of Aeneas, who speaks not one word in the whole *Aeneid*. At least she survives, as do the

Sabine women, tricked along with their men to attend a religious celebration only to be carried off and raped to produce Roman men. Elsewhere death of women, by their own hands or those of their families, looms large in Rome's origin myths. It seems the only honorable way for women to participate in beginnings is to shortly thereafter disappear from the scene.

Lucretia is the archetype: her rape, accusation against King Tarquin the Proud, and suicide are the essential preludes to the Republic.[21] Parallel to the story of Lucretia is that of Verginia, the daughter of Verginius, lusted after by the judge Appius Claudius, the most powerful man in Rome. Claudius arranged for one of his clients, Marcus Claudius, to claim her as his slave and to bring the claim before his court. Her father, unable to resist the powerful judge, asked a moment alone with her, only to plunge his dagger into her heart, telling her, "In only this way, daughter, can I defend your freedom."[22] Just as Lucretia's death gave birth to the Republic, Verginia's death gives birth to law.[23] When Roman women are present at the beginning, they do not live long.

Women in Judeo-Christian Antiquity

Just as important as Greek and Roman representations of women in origin narratives are those of sacred scripture in establishing the place of women at the beginning. The Hebrew Bible's story of Eve and her role as temptress casts a long shadow across the Christian tradition. But as Hans-Werner Goetz has emphasized, Eve was more than merely a temptress.[24] The first woman incorporates all that is essential in women. She is the model of every woman, both in her humanity, which is evidenced by being made of the rib of Adam, and in her natural subordination to him. This subordination, commentators point out, was not the result of her sin but of her essentially subordinate nature: even had she not sinned, she would have been under Adam's authority, although in this case the subordination would have been based on love, not on fear.[25] And yet although subordinate, Eve, and thus all women, share in the essential humanity of Adam and thus in the image of God;[26] if they are socially inferior to men, they are spiritually equal. The unity of Adam and Eve, of man and wife, can even stand as symbol of Christ's love for his Church.

Nevertheless, the sin of Eve, although shared by Adam, remained a heavy burden on the first woman and on all women. Through her weakness, sin entered the world and with sin, death. Eve, the "mother of all the living" (Genesis 4, 20) is also the mother of death.[27]

If Eve was fundamental for the origins of all men and for the essence of all women, other biblical origin stories omit women entirely. Equally important for understanding beginnings are the accounts of the origins of peoples in the book of Genesis and their subsequent commentaries.

Accounts of the descendants of the sons of Noah and the story of the tower of Babel are both crucial to medieval understandings of peoples and languages, but neither mentions any women.[28] The first biblical matriarchs are Sarah and Hagar. Both are mothers of peoples, the Hebrews-Jews, and the Arabs. Their appearance not only in the Bible but in the Qur'ān and in later commentaries, both rabbinical and Muslim, develop a complex intertextual tradition that relates to the developing animosities between Jews and Arabs even before Islam, incorporated into Christian exegesis, and continuing well in to the High Middle Ages.[29]

Mary, the new Eve, presents another, particularly complex issue for Christians. In Christianity, there was no question of eliminating Mary from the origin story: the problem was rather the opposite—how to write her in. Although by the second century she was understood as the only human parent of Jesus in

orthodox Christian tradition, she is not part of either of the genealogies of Jesus presented in the Gospels, both of which end
with Joseph. As exemplar and as model of descent, the complexity of Mary's place in the family of Jesus gave rise to complex
and contradictory reflections on genealogy, descent, and kinship
through the Middle Ages.[30]

Origin Narratives at the End of Antiquity

By the sixth century, then, Greek, Roman, and Jewish traditions had elaborated certain models of origin accounts and certain ways that women might be included, excluded, or compro-
mised within these traditions. Late antique and early medieval
authors reworked their accounts of origins both in terms of these
received traditions and their own circumstances. But while much
has been written about origin legends, the problem of women's
place in origin narratives has only recently begun to be ad-
dressed, specifically by the Austrian scholars Walter Pohl and
Herwig Wolfram, and by them in the specific context of what
are called *origo gentis* texts, that is, narratives that pretend to
recite the origin of a people.[31] However, as both of these scholars
readily point out, *origines gentium* do not exist as a specific genre
in antiquity or in the Middle Ages, although stories of origins,
whether written or oral, were a regular element of many genres.
While one such text, the *Origo gentis Langobardorum*, does indeed carry this title in medieval manuscripts, this circumstance
is virtually unique.[32] More often, origin stories are embedded in
other sorts of texts, and the origins can take a wide variety of
forms. Thus, the account may be the laconic *libri generationum*,
genealogies of Jewish and Christian scripture with their lists of
begats, or the enumeration of ancestors of Anglo-Saxon, Gothic,
or Lombard kings. The gens may be a leading aristocratic or
royal family, *pars pro toto*, in which the whole people is under-

stood somehow to participate. These genealogies, or more elaborate stories, may appear in world histories, in ethnographic excursus, as prefaces to legal collections, even in administrative texts. They may be brief allusions or complex, rhetorically elaborated histories. Their authors may themselves identify with the kindred or people whose origins they recount, but they can also report the origins of peoples or families that the authors identify as foreign to their own identities. Moreover, since the time of Herodotus, the narrator may represent the account as an internal discourse of the family or people, or may represent it as the external account told by others.

At one time, the primary interest of such stories was an attempt to discover in them distant oral traditions of the preliterate histories of European peoples. Herodotus's accounts of the Scyths; Tacitus's *Germania* and *Agricola*; Procopius's *Gothic Wars*; Jordanes's *Getica*; Paulus Diaconus's *Historia Langobardorum*; the texts of Gregory of Tours and Fredegar on the Franks; Widukind of Corvey's *Res gestae Saxonicae*; Constantine Prophyrogennetos's *De administrando imperio*, concerning the Croats, Serbs, and other Slavic peoples; Cosmas of Prague's chronicle; the Gallus Anonymous's account of early Poland; Saxo Grammaticus's *Gesta Danorum*; and other similar authors were scrutinized to discover the original origins of these peoples or at least the authentic voice of folk tradition. This positivist enterprise was particularly developed within the tradition of Germanic philology and mythology. The origins of specifically Germanic peoples became central to the elaboration of Germanic history and ideology, and these stories were seen as key elements in uncovering the authentic voice of Germanic culture.

More recently, this enterprise has drawn criticism from a variety of perspectives. First, the essentialist approach to Germanic origin texts and, indeed, the essential identity of so-called Germanic societies are largely being discarded. Just as there is no specific *origo gentis* genre, there is no specific Germanic form of these stories. It makes no sense to isolate accounts of the Lombards, Goths, Franks, or Danes from accounts of the origins of the Romans, Israelites, Scyths, Huns, Arabs, Czechs, or Poles. Second, one now recognizes that it is not meaningful to distinguish between the origins of "peoples" and those of families. As I've suggested, the origin story of a people may be that of its leading or royal family. Conversely, an account of the origins of a people may be appropriated by a kindred as part of its own identity and tradition. Third, scholars are increasingly aware that much of the apparent "folk" traditions in these texts are actually derived from Latin and Greek ethnographic and historical texts, relegating the search for distant voices of the barbarian world to romantic myth. Rather than attempting to use these texts to uncover the actual early history of peoples or the pre-Christian religious beliefs of barbarian societies, such texts are increasingly studied either in terms of the preoccupations of the authors themselves or as ways of understanding the complexities of their societies at the time that they wrote.[33]

Rather than making these accounts less interesting, however, all of these approaches make them more so, because by expanding the horizons of origin myths beyond the canonical list of Germanic *origines gentium* and by focusing on how they are constructed, one can see their authors imagining the past in terms of the present and making use of complex and often contradictory material, whether it comes from classical or oral tradition, in a new and creative way.

Such an approach is particularly appropriate when looking at women in origin myths. These myths are contradictory and full of unresolved tensions, but as Walter Pohl has written, "The narratives that deal with these tensions are controversial, and their complexity should not be interpreted away."[34] Such tensions are particularly obvious in dealing with the place of women in the origins of peoples.

These tensions derive from a variety of sources. In Christianity, Islam, and Judaism, normative scripture leaves inconsistencies, ambiguities, and unfinished stories that subsequent generations attempt to resolve. Midrashic traditions, whether the rabbinical Midrash itself, apocrypha and exegetical texts in Christianity, or Tafsīr (Qur'ānic exegesis), Ta'rīkh (historiographical works on the pre-Islamic prophets), Qiṣaṣ al-anbiyā' (popular "Tales of the Prophets"), and of course Hadith in Islam, try to come to terms with these troublesome texts, and do so unconsciously in terms of their own societies and cultures. Similarly, more secular authors, as they reflect on oral traditions and the classical historiographical and ethnographical texts that they hope to reconcile, create a kind of secular midrash in the sense of "searching out" the meaning of authoritative texts and traditions, adding, synthesizing, or commenting on parts of these traditions that they find too important to discard but too problematic to simply report.

And women in genealogies tended to be particularly problematic: whence came they? If the *origo* was constructed as descended from a common male ancestor, then the women on whom the genealogy of males begat were necessarily alien and thus possibly threatening to the identity of the *stirps* or *gens*. But if the *gens* took its origin from a woman, or if a ruler could only base his legitimacy on descent from an illustrious lineage though a woman, then to what extent could the representation of the past serve as model for the future? Finally, if the patron or audience of the account consists of high-status women, how will the author deal with women of the past for women of the present?

The responses to this problem vary widely across the *origo gentis* and genealogical literature. Anglo-Saxon origin accounts, be they the genealogies of royal families or the accounts, reflected in Bede and the Anglo-Saxon Chronicle, of the mythical Hengest and Horsa dispense with women altogether.[35] Apparently elaborated within the context of dynastic rivalries on the one hand

and in the model of biblical typologies of a chosen people on the other, founding women had no place in either schema. Even the heroic Judith, who slays Holofernes and saves her people, remains in Anglo-Saxon exegesis and in the Old English *Judith* an ambivalent figure—courageous, chaste, and devout, but also dangerously seductive and problematic in her deadly violence.[36]

Indeed, the most memorable woman in Anglo-Saxon myth is perhaps Grendel's mother in Beowulf. But she is not the only female of monstrous origin to give birth to monsters in early medieval origin legends. According to the Byzantine historian Jordanes writing in the mid-sixth century, the Huns were sprung from Gothic witches, or *Haliurunnae*. Expelled from the people by King Filimer, they consorted with unclean spirits and gave birth to the Huns, "a dwarfed, filthy and weak people, barely human and having no language but one that little resembled human speech."[37] The intention here is clear: to acknowledge some connection between Goths and Huns, which by the sixth century could hardly be denied, but at the same time to demonize the Huns by ascribing their origins to unclean spirits on the one hand and to females expelled from the Goths for exercising illicit power.

If ideology could determine the strategy of depicting female origins as negative, it could also lead to the reverse. The *Origo gentis Langobardorum* is particularly interesting because it begins with two powerful and clever women, Gambara and the goddess Frea, who together conspire to trick Woden into giving Gambara's people victory over their enemies and their new identity through the imposition of the name *Langobardi*. Rather than attempting to see in this extraordinary story evidence of a unique matriarchal tradition among the Lombards, Walter Pohl has shown that the positive position of Gambara is probably the result of patronage: in the early seventh century, Queen Theodelinda took considerable interest in Lombard history. She probably commissioned the lost *Historiola* or "Little History" of the Lombards by Secundus of Trent.[38] The legend of Gambara and Frea quite likely was transmitted to the later, extant accounts by the anonymous author of the *Origo gentis Langobardorum* and to Paulus Diaconus through this early history. Theodelinda's interest was hardly antiquarian: she was a Frankish Bavarian princess. The authority she commanded in Italy in spite of her foreign birth seems to have been based in large part on her descent from the Lombard King Wacho who had led the Lombards into Pannonia a century before. Her husbands probably needed such prestige: Her first husband, Authari, was the first Lombard king after a hiatus of more than a decade and, although he was the son of Cleph, the last king before the long interregnum, Cleph could claim no ancient royal lineage. Similarly, her second husband, Agilulf, had no royal ancestry and, according to Paulus Diaconus, was chosen by Theodelinda to succeed her husband.[39] Theodelinda thus both provided continuity with the ancient Lombard past and cultivated a model of this past that would legitimate the power she drew from it.

The parallels between Gambara and Theodelinda are even more explicit in that, according to the *Origo*, Gambara was the protector of her two sons, Ybor and Aigo. In the same way, Theodelinda was the guardian of her son Adaloald and ruled in his name during his minority.[40]

Likewise, her daughter Gundeperga, also seen by her contemporaries as a Frank, provided important royal legitimacy to her husbands, first Arioald, who took her as wife to secure his accession to the throne, and later Rothari. As Pohl has argued, Gundeperga was probably instrumental in the elaboration of the *Origo gentis Langobardorum*.[41] In both cases, writing about women at the beginning seems to have been very much a project of writing about and for women in the present. Rather than imagining that the accounts of Gambara reflect some ancient and unique matriarchal tradition among the Lombards, they should be seen in the tradition of powerful women examined by Janet Nelson as "protectrices des historiens des dynasties,"[42] with the further proviso that in commissioning and supporting historians of the Lombard kingdom, they were supporting their own positions.

By the time that Paul the Deacon wrote his *History of the Lombards* generations after Theodelinda and Gundeperga, these powerful and positive images of Gambara had become part of Lombard tradition, and Paul was obliged to include them. Nevertheless, lacking the ideological and patronage framework within which the *Origo* had been written, his own attitude toward this material was more than a little skeptical, influenced as it was both by his Christian ideology and by the political circumstances in which he was writing. He distances himself from the story of Gambara and Frea, dismissing it as a "foolish tale," and he ignores the earlier tradition that Gambara ruled along with her sons. And finally, as important as these women are at the beginning, their significance ends abruptly as he continues his tale. The family of Gambara ends for Paul after the reign of her grandson Agelmund, who designated as his successor a boy born of an unnamed prostitute who had been thrown into a pond at birth. Agelmund rescued the infant and named him Lamissio, who ultimately succeeded him. Unlike the sons of Gambara, Lamissio, the new king of the Lombards, was essentially without a mother and had only a foster father: the powerful women of the Lombards remained firmly restricted to the prehistory of the people. As Lisa Bitel comments on Paul's telling of the tale, "whereas once the Lombard people had been dominated by its mothers, now it organized around men, property and their offspring."[43]

From Herodotus to Paul the Deacon, one sees writers cultivating the idol of origins, attempting, through the depiction of beginnings to say something essential about the way the world either should or should not be in their time. What they are emphatically not doing is depicting the world, past or present, as it is. Their constructions and reconstructions of women in these origins betray a tension between transmission and suppression, and these women—whether the mother of the Scyths, Dido, or Gambara—become an integral part of this depiction, allowing for a complex and fascinating world in which authors struggle to make meaningful received and contradictory traditions in terms of contemporary experience and to form them into exemplary and didactic literature. The following chapter will look in more detail at another frequently recurring motif in myths of origin, the depiction of women at the beginning as more powerful and dangerous than men, as Amazons.

Writing Women Out:

Amazons and Barbarians

Well into his history of the Goths, Jordanes, the sixth-century author who claims to be summarizing a lost history by Cassidorus, enters a long excursus on the valor of Gothic women who, according to his tale, were actually the Amazons. He explains that after their menfolk had left on a military expedition, they were drawn into battle by neighbors.[1] Having been taught by their men, they strongly resisted and defeated the enemy. Emboldened by their victory, they chose two among them, Lampeto and Marpesia, as leaders. While Lampeto remained to defend the borders of their own *patria* (a peculiar choice of words under the circumstances), Marpesia led her army of women to conquer Asia. Then follows a long account drawn primarily from Orosius and Justin of the deeds of the Amazons up to the time of Alexander the Great. Jordanes breaks off this narrative abruptly, however, to ask, "Why does an account concerning the men of the Goths pay so much attention to women?"[2] This is indeed an interesting question, but Jordanes himself provides no answer: instead he returns to the great and praiseworthy deeds of men.

Rather than following Jordanes, let us reflect on his question and ask what Amazons are doing not only in this early and widely influential account of the origin of a people but also, as a second point of reference, in the early-twelfth-century account of the origins of the Czechs by Cosmas of Prague.[3] Indeed, Amazons seem to be an integral part of the account of origins of European peoples from at least the sixth to the twelfth centuries. Although most prominent in Jordanes and in Cosmas, they are also present in Paul the Deacon's account of the Lombards,[4] they appear in passing in the so-called *Chronicle of Fredegar*,[5] they are present in Bede's *History of the English Church and People*,[6] and in Adam of Bremen's account of the bishops of Hamburg,[7] and in other origins of medieval peoples. In later, vernacular texts such as those of the Alexander legends, they were stock figures in accounts of antiquity. Our question is, "Why are Amazons an integral part of the origins of peoples?"

Amazons as Goths

Walter Goffart has a simple answer to their presence in Jordanes: Amazons in Jordanes are mostly there for comic relief.[8] Additionally, since he envisions Jordanes's history of the Goths as actually a love story about the marriage of Goths (the female) and Romans (the male) to create a new, unified people, the Amazon strain in the Goths must be extinguished for them to revert to their proper femininity.

An alternative response, not as naive as it may sound, is that there actually were female warriors among the barbarian peoples encountered by the Romans and Byzantines. Thus, as good ethnographers, Roman and post-Roman authors simply described them. We mustn't dismiss this possibility out of hand: Not only do Amazons figure prominently in classical ethnographic accounts and origin legends from the time of Herodotus through the Middle Ages, but Roman accounts of campaigns against Celtic and Germanic enemies regularly mention women on the battlefield. Later, Avar and Slavic armies reportedly included women.[9] Warrior women figure in vernacular oral traditions and emerge in both Scandinavian literature and in Middle High German texts such as the *Nibelungenlied* and histories such as Saxo Grammaticus's *Gesta Danorum*.[10] Finally, archaeological evidence of women buried with weapons occurs widely. In Sauromatian-Sarmatian burials from the sixth to fourth centuries B.C.E., archaeologists have found tombs of women buried with swords and daggers and at least one skeleton of a young woman bow-legged apparently from riding, supplied with a quiver containing forty bronze-tipped arrows, an iron dagger, and hanging around her neck, a leather pouch containing a bronze arrowhead.[11] From the early Middle Ages, some sixteen Avar women's graves were excavated in southern Slovakia that contained none of the usual female ornaments and grave goods but instead horses, normally typical of high-status men.[12] Such finds have led historians and archaeologists to conclude that women in nomadic societies may well have had a military role that led to or reinforced legends of Amazon warrior maidens.

But even if women warriors existed among some barbarian peoples, this is insufficient reason for their considerable place in accounts of the origins of peoples. It is one thing to say that a phenomenon existed. It is quite another to say why of all of the phenomena that existed, one is singled out for extensive description and discussion. Thus, bracketing the question of evidence of the real existence of warrior women, we must ask what our authors were doing with this image in their texts.

Here Walter Goffart was correct to observe that gendered language is part of a wider strategy that is part of an argument, not merely a description. However, Jordanes's argument depended on a received tradition that had already established Amazons as Goths. Yet, Jordanes did not share the ideological perspective that caused this identification in the first place, and thus his report of these warrior women fits awkwardly into his narrative. He isn't sure why they are there himself, as evidenced by both his question and his abrupt abandonment of the Gothic

Amazons. Here he is faithful to a tradition that he does not understand. Subsequent medieval authors such as Cosmas, writing about the origins of peoples, will restore meaning to such accounts, drawing both on Jordanes and on the earlier classical traditions of Amazons to redefine the meaning of these women warriors in the prehistory of their peoples. Our first question then is to understand how Amazons became Goths in the first place, to answer the question Jordanes could not. In other words, how did Amazons appear in barbarian history, and how did they disappear?

As Walter Pohl has remarked, the legend of the Amazons, for all its popularity in traditional historiography, enjoys no fixed meaning: its ambiguity and its inner contradictions kept the story alive, so that many texts are in fact polyphonic and contain traces of controversy on the subject.[13]

One should add that the ambiguity and contradictions of the story also facilitated its strategic employment as a means to address other, even troubling and controversial issues, particularly concerning gender relationships. This can be observed at two key moments in the development of Amazons within European origin myths, the moment when the Amazons became Goths, and the moment when Bohemians became Amazons.

Jordanes had to write about Amazons because he knew, from his reading of the *Historia Augusta* or of others who had read it, as well as from Orosius, that the Amazons were in fact Goths.[14] From the time of Herodotus, Amazons were a stock element in any ethnographic account. For these early historians and ethnographers, however, they existed at the beginning of history, or perhaps just before the beginning of history.[15] They existed on the margins not only of time but also of space: they were initially relegated to distant Anatolia near the river Thermodon, or else in Libya, Thrace, and western Asia Minor, regions peripheral to the Greek world. Interestingly, they were both ferocious warriors and founders of cities. Their story was regularly used to emphasize the failure of men to act properly and the need to reassert appropriate hierarchy: the battle with the Amazons, the *Amazonomachia*, was a violent and erotic restoration of order. However, the existence of the Amazons, and their reappearance in heroic accounts from Heracles to Alexander, perhaps indicated the continuing struggle within Greek society both against the monstrous disorder that a society of warrior women represented and against the equally monstrous solution of female annihilation.

By the third century, however, the chronological and spatial distance separating civilization from a world in which such monstrous women could exist was closing fast. According to the *Historia Augusta*, it closed completely in 271 when Aurelian's legions, crossing the Danube in pursuit of the Goths, killed the Gothic king along with five thousand of his warriors and returned to Rome with Gothic prisoners.[16] The *Historia* continues that in 274, when Aurelian organized his triumph after having reunited the two halves of the empire, he included in the triumph, along with captive rebels and barbarians from the far corners of the realm, "ten women who, dressed in male attire, had been captured fighting among the Goths, after many had died, and whom a placard indicated to be of the gens of the Amazons—for placards indicting the names of their peoples were carried before all."[17]

The vivid description of Aurelian's triumph, which unfortunately Michael McCormick tells us is quite implausible, at least in the extraordinary detail recorded in the *Historia Augusta*, presents the "smoking gun": Gothic women, captured in battle, explicitly identified as living members of the *Gens Amazonum*.[18] What else was Jordanes/Cassiodorus, who knew the text, to think?

But we need to ask what Aurelian, or rather perhaps the author of the *Historia*, was saying with these Amazons. Why should they appear now? We must remember that while we may be interested in the ten Amazons in the triumph, they were only a sideshow in what is, in the account, an enormous spectacle: three royal chariots, twenty elephants, four tigers, giraffes, eight hundred pairs of gladiators, and captive barbarians including Blemmyes, Axomitae, Arabs, Indians, Bactrians, Hibverians, Saracens, Persians, Goths, Alans, Roxolani, Sarmatians, Franks, Suebians, Vandals, and Germans. But the real prizes were Tetricus and his son, the Gallic emperors defeated by Aurelian shortly before, a defeat that ended a long-lasting division of the empire in the west, and, most important, Zenobia, the ruler of Palmyra and the military genius who had led the most successful separatist movement in Roman history. Aurelian's defeat of Tetricus had been a walk in the park: Tetricus could barely maintain his control even while Aurelian was busy in the east, and he surrendered to him quickly when Aurelian turned his attention to the west. But Zenobia was something else: here was a real Amazon queen in all but name. The second wife of Odaenathus of Palmyra, after her husband's death she assumed power in the name of her infant son. She defeated a Roman army sent by Emperor Gallienus and then went on to conquer Syria, Bostra, Egypt, and most of Asia Minor. At first Aurelian had accepted this as a fait accompli, but in 271 Zenobia proclaimed her son Augustus, formally splitting the empire. She destroyed the first army sent against her and finally could be defeated and conquered only by Aurelian himself. She was a warrior who had ruled, according to the *Historia augusta*, "not in feminine fashion or with the ways of a woman, but surpassing in courage and skill, not merely Gallienus, than whom any girl could have ruled more successfully, but also many an emperor . . . Zenobia was ruling Palmyra and most of the East with the vigour of a man."[19]

The author of the *Historia* employs Zenobia in the way that other authors had for centuries used Amazons: the strength of Amazons is the direct result of the failure of men. Concerning Gallienus he writes: "Now all shame is exhausted, for in the weakened state of the commonwealth things came to such a pass that, while Gallienus conducted himself in the most evil fashion, even women ruled most excellently."[20] In the words of Edmond Frézouls, "Rome had reached bottom: the age of Gallienus was the age of sub-men and of Amazons."[21] Nor was Zenobia the only woman whose martial abilities and ambitions shamed the male commanders. The *Historia augusta* asserts that it was Victoria, the widow of the Gallic Emperor Victorinus, who had put Tetricus up to the emperorship in Gaul. The author even claimed that Zenobia told Aurelian that she had written to Victoria, suggesting a partnership in power: a woman ruling the east and another the west. Victoria had died prior to Aurelian's campaign in the west, so she could not be paraded along with Zenobia and the Amazons. Still, the *Historia* presents Aurelian's victory over women in the east, west, and, with the Gothic Amazons, center, in a manner consistent with Aurelian's official title, *Restitutor Orbis*. Restitution of the world means the restitution not only of rebellious provinces of the empire and the defeat of barbarian neighbors: it means the restitution of the proper power relations between men and women. Just as the rule by women had been a sign of the shame into which the empire had fallen, the sight of Amazons and Zenobia in chains meant the restoration of the world. Thus did the Amazons become Goths.

The Amazons and Goths continued to be closely identified in the fifth century, although within a Christian tradition the age of the Amazons did not necessarily mean a time of male weakness. Orosius, writing his apologetic histories, understood the Amazons as Goths, inserting a standard version of their history taken largely from Justinus, the author of what might be called the best-selling Western Civilization textbook in late antiquity.[22] Here they begin as Scythian women whose husbands have been slaughtered by their neighbors. They conquer almost all of Europe and Asia. However, unlike the author of the *Historia augusta*, Orosius breaks with the traditional use of powerful women such as Amazons, namely to emphasize the failure of men to rule with appropriate strength. Indeed, he is even willing to attribute a positive role to Gallia Placidia, the sister of the Emperor Honorius captured by the Goths, in bringing about peace between the barbarians and Romans.[23] In keeping with the polemical direction of his whole work, he connects the power of the Amazons to the blindness of paganism:

> O Grief! The shame of human error! Women, fleeing from their native land, entered, overran, and destroyed Europe and Asia. . . . The blame for the oppression of the times was nevertheless not to be imputed to the utter worthlessness of men.[24]

Rather than evidence of male failure, Amazons are one more symptom of the evils of paganism. Even though he is writing after the sack of Rome by the Visigoths in 410, his presentation of the Goths of his time is of a mild, relatively pacific people compared with their Amazon ancestors. He contrasts the violence of the Amazons to the recent settlement of Goths within the empire, "those men whose wives had destroyed the greater part of the earth with measureless slaughter."[25]

By the sixth century then, Jordanes/Cassidorus, writing about the Goths, had to include the Amazons. However, they had lost the meanings that they had had for earlier authors. Jordanes had no interest in Aurelian and the ideological position of the *Historia augusta*. Nor does he continue the classical tradition of using Amazons to emphasize the degeneracy of male authority in the past. At the same time, he is not contrasting pagan and Christian values as was Orosius. But because he found Amazons among the Goths, just as he had found them among Orosius's Scythians, they had to appear in his history of the Goths.[26] Here again they arise because of a vacuum of male leadership. However, the men are away on an expedition, not annihilated by their neighbors. While the Gothic army is away, a neighboring people attempts to carry off their women. The rest of his account closely follows Orosius and Justinus but necessarily becomes lost in the history of the Goths. Amazons do not, after all, make for good ancestors, as they either kill or send away their male offspring.[27] Jordanes thus cannot bring his Gothic Amazons into the origins of the Goths again. After his abrupt question of why he is even writing about them, he abandons them for the rest of his text.

Jordanes's Amazons remain a largely unintegrated element in his history of the Goths. But through his text, and through similar use of his sources, Amazons reappear in a wide spectrum of subsequent histories of peoples. They do so, however, as in Jordanes, at the beginning, or even before the beginning, of the people, and their defeat or destruction marks the beginning or reconstitution of the proper order of the world.

Czechs as Amazons

The place of Amazons in the origin account of the Bohemians or Czechs illustrates the increasing complexity of the subsequent instrumentalization of the topos of early Amazons in the early history of a people. By the time that Cosmas of Prague wrote his Bohemian chronicle at the start of the twelfth century, Amazons had become necessary characters in virtually any prehistory of a people. Cosmas however, unlike Jordanes, restores them to their antique role of social criticism, but with a unique twist.

The whole chronicle follows the history of Bohemia and its Premysl dynasty until the year of Cosmas's death, 1125.[28] It begins, in a manner common to other such histories, with the story of the tower of Babel, and then moves to Europe and a region he calls *Germania*, flowing with milk and honey but devoid of people. The first humans to enter the region are lead by Boemus, after whom his followers name the region. The first generations lived in a prelapsarian paradise, when no one knew the word *meum* but only *nostrum*.[29] This was also an age of gender equality:

> At that time the virgins of this land came to maturity without control [*sine iugo*] and carried arms like Amazons and, choosing commanders for themselves, fought just like young male soldiers and penetrated into the forests to hunt in a manly way, and they did not allow themselves to be chosen by men, but they chose whom and when they wanted, and like the Scythians men and women did not wear different dress."[30]

This paradise did not last, and communal property ceded to private, as conflict and injustice entered this society. Still, there were neither judges nor princes, and when people had conflicts, they spontaneously brought them to those persons who were in morals and honor deemed to be the greater. Among these was one Crocco, whose reputation for dispute settlement was such that people from far and near came to him to settle their conflicts. At his death Crocco left no sons, but rather three daughters. And here our story begins.

The first two daughters were Kazi and Tetka. Kazi was another Media of Kolchis, universally acclaimed for her skills with plants and medicinal incantations.[31] Tetka, the second daughter, was equally praised for her sharp intelligence.[32] However, she taught the ignorant people to adore deities and instituted sacrilegious rites. The youngest daughter, Libuše, was the most marvelous of the three: wise in council, powerful in speech, chaste in body, outstanding in morals, second to none in her concern for justice, affable to all, a glory and decoration of the female sex. But, Cosmas adds, "since no one is in every way good, this praiseworthy woman—oh sad human estate—was a *phitonissa*, that is, a seer.[33]

Libuše is a complex character who both fascinates and repels Cosmas. She was so universally beloved that she was made the judge of all quarrels. But it happened that two wealthy men came before her to settle a property dispute. She lay, "as is the wanton softness of women when they do not have a man whom they might fear, on her elbow on her soft and richly decorated bed."[34] She judged the case justly without regard to the persons, and gave her verdict. The one who lost, however, complained that it was an intolerable injury that a woman should render justice. "We know that a woman, either standing or seated on a throne understands little, so how much less must she understand lying in a bed. A bed is more suited to receiving a husband than speaking martial justice." He goes on to exclaim that it would be better for men to die than to accept female rule and that such as they, meaning the Czechs, are cut off from other nations and peoples because they lack a ruler and virile severity.[35]

Libuše, hiding her shame and anger, admitted that she was and would remain a woman and that since she did not judge them with an iron rod, and since they did not live in terror, they rightly despised her. "For where there is fear, there is honor. Now you need a rector who is stronger than a woman."[36] With this she sent them home and told them that whomever they would choose the next day as lord, she would accept as husband. But that night she called together her two sisters to divine the future by their magical arts. The next day, after she had warned the people of the dangers of having a duke ("O you unfortunate people, who do not know how to live free, and that no good person loses freedom except along with life"), she continues her famous caution against princes, largely drawn from the first book of Kings and from Sallust; extols the value of liberty; and catalogs the impositions and demands that would be made by a ruler on their sons and daughters, even on the livestock.[37] Yet, the people persist in their demand for a duke, and she indicates to them that they will find a man in the village of Staditz on the banks of the Bila, plowing with two oxen. This man, whose name was Premysl, would be the first of the Premysl dynasty. "His name in Latin means thinking thoughts out or outsmarting. His children will rule all this land forever and beyond."[38] Emissaries did as they were told, found Premysl, and brought him back to marry Libuše, assume the position of duke, and, again through her prophetic powers, identify and found the city of Prague.

Cosmas's text has long been the object of scholarly attention, either as evidence of pre-Christian Slavic religion, of distant memories of matriarchy among the west Slavs, or simply as an elaborate critique of the Czech dukes of Cosmas's time.[39] One can also ask about the extent to which this account reflects social and cultural reality: some see the account of Libuše as confirming that female seers accompanied Slavic armies in the eleventh and twelfth centuries. This is certainly not impossible, as one accompanied a Polish army as late as 1209.[40] Were there women warriors in Slavic or other Central and Eastern European societies? As fascinating as these questions about the reflection of reality in the text may be, they are not ours. Instead, our purpose is to consider how Cosmas attempts to make sense of inherited traditions, whether Czech and local or classical and universal; how his text is a sort of midrash, searching out the meaning of Libuše for his day and his audience.

If the much-debated *Legenda Christiani* indeed dates from the tenth century, then Cosmas may be elaborating on a tradition at least two hundred years old. According to this text, the Slavs of Bohemia lived like an unbridled horse, without law, prince, or city until, stricken by a plague, they turned to a certain *phitonissa* for divination and advice. Having received her counsel, they established the city of Prague. Then, still following her advice, they found a wise and prudent man named Premysl, whose occupation was agriculture, and appointed him prince or ruler, joining him in matrimony to the *phitonissa*.[41]

If this was the bare tradition received by Cosmas, we can follow how he transformed it, elaborating a story that preserved its essentials while transforming the meaning into a commentary on the relationship between ruler and people. Central to this transformation is Libuše, a carefully constructed figure whose story is deeply informed by Cosmas's reading of classical texts, among them Ovid, Horace, Stacius, Virgil, and the Bible (especially the Acts of the Apostles and the critique of kingship in the first book of Kings), but also Boethius, Sedulius, Regino of Prüm, and other early medieval authors.[42] Cosmas's Libuše is not a naively reported figure from Slavic folklore: whatever her distant origins, in his text she recalls in particular the female judges of the Bible—especially Deborah, "who used to sit under a palm tree and the people of Israel came up to her for judgment—and at the same time a *phitonissa*, or medium. Again, this tradition is complex and recalls both the Sybiline oracles and the *phitonissa* to whom a desperate King Saul turned for knowledge of the future. The resulting image is anything but the simple reporting of traditions concerning Libuše and Premysl.

Clearly, he is extremely ambivalent about Libuše. On the one hand she is the paragon of female virtue and demonstrates herself superior to the men of her time. She is, with Premysl, the ancestor of the Bohemian dukes, including Duke Vladislav I (1109–17 and 1120–25). Her judgment, like her prognostications, is true. And yet, he constantly disparages her softness, her lack of a male to control her, and most significantly he characterizes her and her sisters as furies. They practice the magic arts, and she is, he says twice, a *phitonissa*, a seer. He compares her to the Cumaean Sybil.[43]

The term *phitonissa* is perhaps the way into a deeper understanding of the tensions and problems within the person of Cosmas's Libuše. *Phitonissa* is a medieval variant of *pythonissa*, a term derived from Pythia, the high priestess who uttered the responses of the Delphic Apollo. She was in term named for the Python, the vast serpent slain near Delphi by Apollo and well known to Cosmas from Ovid's *Metamorphoses*. Like Hercules' Scythian consort or Melusine, the snake woman who is the mother of the Lusignan family, there is perhaps something serpentine about her.

Moreover, the choice of *phitonissa*, rather than the more positive *prophetessa* or some more classical choice such as *vates*, has a specific resonance: the term is postclassical. It first appears in Jerome's translation of the *Vulgate* and refers to the medium consulted by King Saul in 1 Chronicles 10, 13, referred to as a *mulier habens pythonum* in 1 Samuel 28, that is, a woman possessed. But is Libuše possessed? Cosmas does not explicitly say so. However, like the Hebrew medium who summons the ghost of the prophet Samuel, Libuše, as a wielder of magical arts, is a transgressor of divine order intimately involved with kingship and royal succession. And yet, like Libuše, the *pythonissa* summoned by Saul is not an altogether negative figure: first she attempts to refuse the royal request, just as Libuše attempted to reject the people's demand that she find them a duke. After Saul faints from hunger and fear at the announcement of his imminent death, she kills her fatted calf for him and cajoles him into taking some nourishment. Peter Damien, in a letter to Abbot Desiderius of Montecassino, praises the *phitonissa* (he uses the same rare spelling as Cosmas) for returning good for evil.[44]

Moreover, both women prophesy the truth: the spirit of Samuel (or rather, according to most medieval commentators, a phantasm of Samuel) accurately predicts the death of Saul the next day. Libuše too predicts the truth: she finds the future duke, the city of Prague, and even foresees the Bohemian saints Wenceslas and Adalbert.[45] She exercises occult powers, but she does so with justice and in pursuit of truth. This paradox of female authority that is somehow illegitimate (or perhaps paralegitimate) and yet positive hovers over Cosmas's whole chronicle.

At the same time that Libuše is arranging the future of the Premysls and founding Prague, the Bohemian Amazons are establishing nearby their own city, Devin, the city of the virgins. The young men, unable to conquer the city by force, resort to stealth: under the guise of peace they enter the city of the virgins for a feast but in the night rise up, rape and carry off the girls, and burn Devin.

Significantly, as Herwig Wolfram has pointed out,[46] the foundation account ends with the defeat and capture of the warrior maidens by the young men and concludes: "And from that time forward, after the death of Princess Libuše, our women are subject to the authority of men."[47] In a very real sense, then, Libuše and the Amazons belong not to the history of the Bohemian lands but to their prehistory. Her death and their defeat are preconditions for the start of history.

However, Cosmas's emplotment of the Amazons does not simply adopt the classical tradition on which it draws. Unlike the *Amazonomachia*—or indeed the grizzly slaughter in the Czech language, the *Dalimil Chronicle* of 1314—the violence is restrained: the Amazons are not killed; they are married, albeit with the violence of rape. The foundation of male rule is thus more reminiscent of the Roman rape of the Sabine women than the destruction of the Amazons. Nor is Libuše destroyed or even condemned. Her power may be suspect, but she works for the good of society. This is in a real sense Cosmas's dilemma: woman's power may not conform to the proper order of the world, but it both can be potent and can advance the cause of justice.

This is the same dilemma that he faces when dealing with the most powerful woman of his day. For just as the author of the *Historia Augusta* wrote of Amazons when he really was concerned about the queen of Palmyra, when Cosmas wrote about Libuše and the Bohemian Amazons, he was reflecting on Mathilda of Tuscany, another woman who exercised judgment and settles disputes in his chronicle.[48] Cosmas's description of her could almost fit Libuše: she rules Lombardy and Burgundy after the death of her father, "having the power to elect and to enthrone or to dismiss 120 bishops."[49] Not only was Mathilda the woman who most famously brought about the temporary reconciliation of Pope Gregory VII and Emperor Henry IV at Canossa, but equally important from Cosmas's perspective, she reconciled Cosmas's patron Bishop Jaromir of Prague (d. 1090) and his brother the duke and later King Vratislav (1061–92) and brought about the former's restoration to his see. Here, as in the case of Libuše, Cosmas confronts the positive effects of female power. At the same time, he reports an apocryphal story in which Mathilda is accused of using *malificium* to prevent Duke Welf of Suabia from performing his marital duties on their wedding night. Again, one sees the uneasy combination of virtue and magic.[50]

However, in Cosmas's text, Libuše and the Amazons are much more than simply figures of Mathilda. Unlike Jordanes, Cosmas, well educated in the classical tradition at Liège, understood that Amazons flourish in times when men are not ruling as they should. And yet his point about Libuše and the Amazons is not to characterize simply the necessary dominance of men even over competent, virtuous women but rather to gender the Bohemian people as feminine and thus in need of a strong ruler. The age of Libuše prefigures the future relationship between the Bohemian populace and its dukes: lordship is harsh, its powers coercive and destructive. And yet without lords, societies, like women without husbands, are prey to their own weaknesses. Even the best woman must cede power to men; even the Bohemians must accept the power of their dukes.

Still, Cosmas is no run of the mill medieval misogynist. Libuše may represent the need of the Bohemians for ducal control, but she remains both a figure of justice and guidance to her people and her husband. Just perhaps this is in part owing to Cosmas's own situation: although a canon of the Cathedral of Prague and a deacon, he was married and had at least one son, Henry. His wife Bozeteha died in 1117 shortly before he finished the first section of his chronicle, and he remembered her in book 3 as "the inseparable companion in all my undertakings."[51] Of course, before we assume this to be simply the outpouring of his grief and recognition of his wife's equality and companionship, we must recognize that the line is itself a reminiscence of a poem attributed to Prosper of Aquitaine that begins: "Age iam precor mearum comes irremota rerum."[52] Thus his wife, no less than Libuše, becomes an intertextual reference. And yet in the crafting of this epitaph, no less than in the crafting of his women at the beginning of his chronicle, we can recognize an elderly man using gendered categories to criticize his contemporaries, warn his ruler, and remember his wife.

In conclusion, we see how malleable was the motif of Amazons at the origins of peoples: Although firmly established as part of the prehistory of peoples, what this prehistory meant could change. It could be employed to criticize weak lordship, but it could also criticize a society that because of its failings needed stern authority. As its uses shifted with different social and cultural motivations, the texture of misogyny also varied: Cosmas is much less unambiguously opposed to the public role of women than most previous or subsequent authors. His powerful women belonged, unlike those of the third century, to a world that was genuinely attractive even if it, in the end, had to be destroyed in order for divinely willed order to be created.

Libuše and the Czech Amazons may have been legendary, but not only legendary women could be relegated to the prehistory of families and dynasties. The following chapter traces the progressive effacement of two very real and very powerful women to whom subsequent generations of males owed their status and power.

CHAPTER THREE

A Tale of Two Judiths

If mythical women stood at the beginnings of origin legends, this may be because real flesh-and-blood women stood at the beginnings of great aristocratic families. After all, such families of the twelfth and thirteenth centuries largely owed their status, their lands, and their power to women. As Constance Bouchard and before her Karl Ferdinand Werner have pointed out, the great comital families might often appear to spring from "new men" in the ninth or tenth centuries, but actually these new men owed their rise to fortuitous marriages with greater, established families.[1]

Family chroniclers and genealogists were well aware of the importance of such marriages in preserving and augmenting family power and honor—it was a constant and essential element in generational strategies throughout the Middle Ages. As Anita Guerreau-Jalabert has argued, the image of a strictly agnatic descent through generations is more an invention of nineteenth-century genealogists than a reflection of medieval perceptions of kinship.[2] At the same time, the question of how much credit for the successes of kindreds should be attributed to these women rather than to the men of the kindred remained very much in question. As Janet Nelson points out, elite women played a double symbolic role within their husbands' lineages: first, they made possible the continuation of the lineage, but at the same time, because they did not themselves belong to it, they made possible the individualization of a particular offspring within the lineage.[3] Thus reconstruction of family histories meant coming to terms, under differing needs and circumstances, with the relative importance of such marriages and of the women who put not only their dowries and their bodies but their personalities and kinsmen to work on behalf of their husbands and their children. Over time, the ideological imperative of illustrious male descent could best be fostered if memory of the women who made their rise possible was removed from center stage in favor of the audacious acts of men.

In the ninth century, two great families arose because of two women named Judith—a fortuitous name that recalled the widow who, during the siege of Jerusalem by the Assyrians, saves her city by pretending to offer herself to Holofernes only to behead him and return in triumph to her people.[4] The biblical Judith was thus, as Heide Estes has pointed out, one of the few models of a woman playing an active role in public life available, although the reception of the story of Judith in the Middle Ages shows the dangerous ambiguity attached to this woman.[5] The younger of the Judiths considered in this chapter was the granddaughter of the elder, and their stories illustrate the two principal ways that women could be at the start of families' fortunes. The story of how these beginnings were reformed over time suggests the complexities of aristocratic dynastic memory in the tenth through twelfth centuries.

Empress Judith

The first Judith illustrates how the marriage of a daughter to a king or great aristocrat raised the status of her father and brothers. With the marriage, the family achieved a proximity to the king, her brothers and cousins became part of the royal inner circle, forming a powerful faction at court. This was especially true when the queen was a forceful and competent figure, using her traditional role as manager of the royal household and her influence with her husband and, eventually, her son, on behalf of her kin. Such women could well be considered founding mothers. The greatest example of such an ascent through the marriage of a daughter to a king was that of the Welfs, the most powerful noble lineage in the Staufer Empire.[6]

The Welfs are also one of the most precocious families in terms of their interest in their origins. Already in the early twelfth century, the family had a notion of their origins and identity in written form. By the end of the century, this family's sense of its past was integral not only to its image of its contemporary power but also to its claims to royal power. First studied in a pioneering article by Karl Schmid in 1968,[7] the Welfs and their genealogical literature have been a touchstone of subsequent investigations of the representation of genealogical consciousness in the medieval aristocracy.[8] As a result, they are an ideal vehicle through which to examine an aristocratic family's memory of the women who were largely responsible for its fortunes.

The first known Welf was already a powerful figure in the first half of the ninth century, characterized by the biographer of Louis the Pious, Thegan, as being "from the most noble kindred of the Bavarians."[9] This was not, however, exactly true. The eighth-century redaction of the Laws of the Bavarians lists the five most important *genealogiae* or kindreds of the Bavarians whose status stood just below the ducal Agilufings. Welf and his family are not among them, although they may have already formed marriage alliances with some of these key Bavarian clans.[10] One can more honestly conclude that they were a family on the rise, lacking the truly illustrious ancestry of the Agilufings or Huosi, but moving up in the new social order of the Carolingian world.[11] They may have been relatively recently established in Bavaria, with deeper roots in Alemannia or in the old

Frankish Austrasian heartland from which the Carolingians themselves had arisen.[12] In any event, this Welf himself had married Heilwig, a member of an aristocratic Saxon family.[13] His kindred were clearly part of the great imperial aristocracy, with lands and power throughout the eastern portions of the Carolingian world. But the alliance that moved this kindred to the very center of the Frankish stage was the marriage of Judith, daughter of Welf and Heilwig, to the emperor Louis the Pious in 819, following the death of Louis's first wife, Irmingard. Judith, according to the *Annales regni Francorum* and the account of an anonymous biographer of Louis known as the Astronomer, was selected in a sort of beauty pageant, in which the emperor examined daughters of the nobility before making his choice, a practice some have seen as imitating Byzantine tradition.[14] More recently, Mayke de Jong has pointed out that this description, and particularly that of the "Astronomer," is less a reflection of Byzantine court tradition than an image of Judith modeled on the biblical figure of Esther, a comparison already made by Hrabanus Maurus in his defense of the empress.[15] Certainly Louis was not simply choosing a beauty queen: he was allying himself with Judith's father and his family. That this marriage was such an alliance is demonstrated by a second royal marriage that shortly followed. Sometime between 825 and 827, Hemma, the sister of the Empress Judith, married the emperor's son by his first marriage, Louis the German, king in East Francia and Bavaria. Finally, Konrad the Elder, brother of Judith and Hemma, married Adelheid, the sister-in-law of Louis the Pious's son Lothar I. The marriage of Judith thus marked the ultimate achievement of a great family—an unprecedented alliance with the Carolingians—and the start of ever closer relations with the royal house.

As mother of Charles the Bald, Judith played a more active, public role than any previous Carolingian queen, intervening on behalf of her favorites and devoting her energies to assuring the future of her son. She was also the channel for imperial favor, which allowed her brothers and other relations to win offices and lands from the king, both in the West Frankish kingdom of Charles and more widely in Alemannia, Bavaria, Raetia, Burgundy, and Lothringia. One relative acquired control over the most important monasteries in West Francia, while others established their power over Auxerre, Sens, St. Maurice d'Agaune, Jumiéges, St. Riquier, and Valenciennes. Judith was no passive figure in the reign of her husband and soon became the target of the hatred and aggression launched by Louis's older sons in response to his desires to carve out a kingdom for Charles the Bald.[16]

As the Carolingian Empire fragmented, most of the near-term advantages gained by the Welfs proved short-lived, although one grandnephew of Judith, Rudolf, attained the kingship of Burgundy in 888 and established a kingdom that endured for several generations. Elsewhere, particularly in Swabia, the Welfs kept a lower profile but continued to consolidate their lands and especially their relationships with important monastic foundations.[17]

A woman thus played a crucial role in the origin and destiny of the Welfs. Judith, through her marriage and through her continuing influence on her husband, established the foundations, however discontinuous, that would allow the Welfs in the eleventh and twelfth centuries to return to the center of the European stage. While in the post-Carolingian period the family retained lands and local power in Swabia, the Welfs disappeared from imperial and royal power, although they gradually built their lordship around Altdorf/Ravensburg and demanded ducal status in competition with the Staufer. Around 1120, a second Welf Judith wed Duke Frederick II of Swabia in an attempt to put an end to these great families' rivalry. She bore Frederick Barbarossa, who, although celebrated as the "cornerstone" to end the conflicts between the two families, ultimately continued the conflict with Henry the Lion as the representative of the great ducal family.

The Welfs took a precocious interest in their family history, being among the first nonroyal families whose origins and genealogies were recorded in their house monasteries, presumably drawing on both written records and family memories and focusing on the formal, liturgical *memoria* of family members. The result is the existence of three twelfth-century genealogical accounts of the family's origins and history that allow us to see how Judith was remembered within the family. The earliest, the *Genealogia Welforum*, was written in the Swabian monastery of Weingarten sometime before the death of Duke Henry the Black of Bavaria in 1126.[18] The second, the so-called Saxon Welf source is now lost in its original form but can be reconstructed from later texts, in particular a supplement to the *Saxon World Chronicle* composed in the 1130s at St. Michael's monastery at Lüneberg, which represents a Saxon version of Welf memory.[19] The third is the *Historia Welforum Weingartensis*, produced around 1170 in upper Swabia.[20] Together these three texts allow one to follow the reflections of various members of the Welf kindred across time as they reflect on their origins and the relative importance of their ancestors in securing their power and status.

The authors of these three texts do not ignore women in the history of the family. Marriage alliances and mothers of significant Welfs are regularly reported. And yet, while these women are present, their presence and their importance is strictly circumscribed, even undercut, by the manner in which they are treated. This is particularly true for the woman whose marriage and subsequent role was paramount for the Welf family, the first Judith, wife of Louis the Pious.

The first record of the Welf family history distorts and undermines the role of the pivotal Judith. First, Judith herself has disappeared entirely. Although the typology of the Judith story remains, it is a fictional one. The laconic *Genealogia* records simply: "Eticho sired a son Henry and a daughter Hiltigard. The Emperor Louis the Stammerer received Hiltigard as wife. Henry made himself the man of the Emperor. His father established twelve monks in Ammergau and there he died."[21] In this earliest version of a family origin myth, all memory of the great figures of the ninth century, including Judith and her father Welf, thus disappear in favor of a legend that ties the origin of the family to a relatively obscure Swabian noble and a marriage that never took place.

The second text, written in Saxony and drawing no doubt on Carolingian historiography, restores Judith to the story (and likewise the first Welf, here given the double name Eticho Welf, indicating that in the oral traditions within the kindred the memory of Eticho remained powerful). And yet, this time Judith's role is undercut in yet another manner. In this account, the Eticho Welf is the father of Judith, "whom Louis [the Pious] took in marriage after the death of Empress Irmingarde and of whom he begot Caesar Charles the Bald."[22] Notice how passive Judith appears in this description: she is taken as wife and of her is generated Charles. She does make an important contribution to the future of the Welf family, however, by counseling her brother to become the vassal of Louis. But this counsel splits her family and could have destroyed their honor. Her father, Welf, is characterized as a prince of highest freedom who would never submit to anyone for a fief, even to the emperor, and orders his son Henry to refuse as well. However Henry, "by the persuasion of his sister Judith" agreed to become the vassal of Louis for a fief of the size that he could circumnavigate at noon with a plow. Welf was said to be so opposed to his daughter's proposition, tantamount to abandoning the family's freedom and honor, that he left Bavaria with twelve followers and lived out the remainder of his life in self-imposed exile with them in the area of Scharnitzwald, never again to see his son or his daughter.

Ultimately Henry triumphed, but he did so not through the marriage of his sister with Louis but in spite of it—through his own cleverness (*caliditate sua*). Concealing a small golden plow on his person, and setting out in advance relays of fresh horses at regular intervals, he set off at a furious pace while the emperor was taking his noonday nap and quickly rode around a vast amount of territory. When the emperor awoke, Henry demanded that he honor his bargain and invest him with the enormous territory that he had claimed. Louis was indignant that he had been tricked, but remembering his promise, had no choice but to grant Henry this vast territory, which formed the core of the Welf's lands in the future.

The story of "Henry of the Golden Plow" both writes Judith into the memory of the Welf's first rise to prominence and at the same time minimizes her role in this rise. Her marriage to Louis is important, but from the perspective of the anonymous Saxon annalist, it is also fraught with danger. Rather than promoting the interests of her family, she urges their subservience to her husband. Only Henry's cleverness prevents, or perhaps mitigates, this dishonor. True, he is still the vassal of the emperor, but he is also lord of a vast territory that he has won, not through his sister's intervention, but through trickery. Having been able to dupe his lord, his position as vassal is hardly one of humble obedience.[23] Henry has in a sense triumphed not only over Louis but over his sister as well.

Subsequently, Judith remains in the family's memory, but not a principal actor in its history. In the *Historia Welforum*, and representing, as Karl Schmid showed, tradition of the upper Swabian Welf court, Judith's role is entirely marginal:

> Welf sired a son named Eticho and a daughter Judith. Louis the emperor, known as the Pious, took this Judith as wife after the death of his wife Irmingard, from whom he had produced three sons, Lothar, Pipin and Louis. From her he sired Charles the Bald, who obtained the kingdom of the Franks in the division of the empire, and who ruled strenuously for forty-five years while his brothers Lothar and Louis reigned in Italy and in Alemannia, after the third brother, Pipin, had died.[24]

In this version, then, Eticho is the son of Welf and the brother of Judith. The opportunity to become the vassal of the emperor does not arise in this generation at all, but in the next. Eticho in turn sires Henry and, when his son swears fealty to the emperor, retires to the forest and founds the monastery of Amberg. Judith has no role at all in the events leading up to the land acquisition and thus the foundation of the Swabian Welfs' territorial lordship.

Judith of Flanders

The memory of Empress Judith shows the transformation of a family's memory of its rise facilitated by a marriage into a royal family. A more common marriage alliance that facilitated a family's advancement was the union of a man of lower status with a woman of higher status. As Georges Duby argued years ago, women marry down, men marry up: these higher-status marriages could launch or consolidate a kindred's position. Everyone was aware of the implications of such a marriage, the "rule of play," as Gerd Althoff would term such implicit but clearly established norms.[25] Marriages of royal daughters were not entered into lightly: Charlemagne went so far as to forbid his daughters to marry, preferring to tolerate their informal alliances and a growing number of bastard grandchildren rather than elevate their aristocratic lovers and their kindreds by the contracting of a formal marriage alliance.

Normally, when such a marriage took place, it was part of a negotiation with the higher-status family: a daughter given in marriage could be a reward for past support as well as a guarantee of support in the future. But this was not always the case. In the most dramatic case of the ninth century, the similarly named granddaughter of the Empress Judith brought the family of the counts of Flanders into royal proximity but in a striking way:

the Count of Flanders eloped with Judith, the daughter of
Charles the Bald, risking all to achieve an alliance, however unwilling, with the royal family.

The story is dramatic and complex. Judith had been married
twice previously. Her first marriage in 856, when she was about
twelve years old, had been arranged by her father and was a
calculated match of royal strategy. Charles gave her to King
Æthelwulf of Wessex (reigned 839–58), a powerful warrior king
who had been widowed and was on the Continent returning
from a pilgrimage to Rome when he and Charles met and con-
tracted the marriage. The union came at a moment of internal
and external danger for the Carolingian. Western counts, an-
gered by Charles's grants to his son Louis the Stammerer of important parts of Neustria, had revolted, rallying around his other
son, Charles of Aquitaine. At the same time, Viking raiders, possibly in coordination with the rebels, sailed up the Seine and
plundered the cities, monasteries, and estates. Charles the Bald
probably hoped that this alliance with the Wessex dynasty would
bring him assistance against both of these threats.[26]

In any event, he saw to it that following the marriage Arch-
bishop Hincmar of Reims consecrated and crowned Judith, and
his new son-in-law, contrary to West Saxon tradition, conferred
on her the title of queen.[27] King Æthelwulf died shortly after, and
his successor and son by a previous marriage, King Æthelbald,
hoping to maintain the alliance, immediately married his step-
mother. This alliance proved ephemeral as well: Æthelbald died
in 860. The twice-widowed Judith then returned to the Continent, where her father sent her to Senlis, according to the *Chronicle of St. Bertin,* "under his protection and royal and episcopal
guardianship, with all the honour due to a queen, until such
time as, if she could not remain chaste, she might marry in the
way the apostle said, that is suitably and legally."[28] Presumably,
Charles was waiting to arrange another advantageous marriage
for his daughter. However, the royal and episcopal guardians

must not have been very vigilant: Judith ran off with Baldwin, a count whose county included at that time merely a narrow band along the coast from Bruges to the mouth of the River Aa.

Generally, Baldwin is credited with the initiative in this audacious gamble, and no doubt this is largely true.[29] However, as Janet Nelson has pointed out, the most comprehensive contemporary source, the *Annals of St. Bertin*, make Judith the actor in the elopement, not simply the passive victim of bride theft: "Charles now learned that she had changed her widow's clothing and gone off with Count Baldwin, at his instigation and with her brother Louis's consent."[30] This description suggests that Baldwin was acting in alliance with Louis, and one may presume that Judith was the reward for Baldwin's support. However, the way that the *Annals* describe Judith's own role suggest that perhaps, after two previous forced marriages, although only sixteen-years-old, the queen may have been ready to take her fate in her hands, seeking out a match that would remove her from the role of pawn in her father's political strategies and provide her with greater personal autonomy than would a marriage with another king.

It was a dangerous gamble: her father was furious—at Baldwin, at Judith, and no doubt at Louis. At his demand, Pope Nicholas I excommunicated the couple. Baldwin and Judith rushed to Rome and brought their cause directly to the pontiff. In time they managed to convince him to rescind the excommunication and even to intervene on their behalf with Charles. After two years, urged by the pope and pressured by the Viking chief who controlled Frisia, Charles finally accepted the elopement as a fait accompli and permitted Judith to marry the count. As Baldwin had hoped, the royal marriage alliance brought with it more than just a bride. He received from Charles the county of Flanders (a smaller area than the Flanders of the High Middle Ages), and in time Ternois, the area of Waas, and the lay abbacy of St. Pieter of Ghent.[31] Baldwin proved a fairly faithful vassal to Charles, although he carefully maintained his relations with Charles's son, who had defied his father by countenancing the elopement and marriage in the first place.

Shortly after Baldwin's death in 879, his son Baldwin II was forced to flee a furious Viking onslaught, abandoning most of his lands. Although he married Aelfthryth, the daughter of King Alfred the Great, he seems to have been willing to cooperate with the Danes when advantageous, only going on the offense when they left the region. Gradually Baldwin II managed to reconquer his paternal inheritance and even expand his holdings, establishing his countship over an enlarged "Flanders" that included not only the *pagi* of Ghent and Waas but Mempisc, Courtrai, the Ijzer, Ternois, Boulonnais, and much of the Tournaisis.[32] By his death in 918, he had created an extensive territorial principality independent of royal control.

In a real sense, then, Baldwin II might be seen as the founder of the family's fortunes. Initially, however, his parents' marriage loomed large in the memories of the descendants of Baldwin and Judith as the foundation story of the dynasty. The earliest account, written by Witger between 951 and 959 and preserved in the great Flemish monastery of St. Bertin, emphasizes the royal descent of the family through Judith.[33] It begins with a genealogy of the Carolingians to the children of Charles the Simple, derived from the *Genealogia Fontanellensi*.[34] Then its rubrics announce, "Here begins the holy race of the most glorious lord Count Arnulf [I "The Great" 918–65] and his son Baldwin [III, d. 962], whom the Lord deign to protect in this world."[35] The genealogy then starts, not with Baldwin I, but with Judith, who had been introduced in the previous, Carolingian genealogy as the daughter of Charles the Bald and Ermentrudis: "Which most prudent and beautiful Judith the most powerful Count Baldwin joined to himself in the bonds of matrimony." It then continues, "From her he engendered a son, bestowing on him the same name as his own, that is Baldwin."[36] Nothing is said of Judith's status as an Anglo-Saxon queen, only as a Carolingian. Baldwin II's marriage is recorded, but not the name of his wife Aelfthryth or her father Alfred, only that she was "from the most noble race of the trans-maritime kingdom." Nor is anything said of Baldwin I's own parentage. He emerges only with his marriage to the royal family, a relationship emphasized later in the genealogy when, recounting Arnulf's pious donations, he reminds his readers that the monastery of Saint-Corneille in Compiègne to which he was particularly generous "had been founded by his great-great-grandfather Charles the Bald." Clearly, it was Judith whom Witger wished to emphasize as he recounted the origins of the counts. For Witger, the comital family began with the marriage of Judith and Baldwin. In the tenth century, the family's Carolingian origins were clearly at the center of their dynastic concerns, and Judith was their source.[37]

By the early twelfth century, when the second Flemish genealogy was written at St. Bertin, the family no longer began with Judith and her marriage to Baldwin. Judith is still present and still the daughter of Charles the Bald, but the family's origins start two generations earlier with one Lidricus, count of Harlebeke. He in turn was the father of Ingelram, the father of Audacer, who is said to be the father of Baldwin.[38] These shadowy figures from the first half of the ninth century certainly existed, although what their relationship to each other was and whether they were indeed the ancestors of Baldwin is quite uncertain. What matters for the genealogist is that Baldwin was not the first of his lineage, and thus his marriage did not create the family. Nor is his marriage with Judith particularly emphasized in the text. His is but the first of a series of marriages with royalty. The marriage of Baldwin II is described in exactly the same terms as that of his father, even if the author erred both on the name of the Anglo-Saxon king and his daughter: "Audacer begat Baldwin Iron Arm who married the daughter of Charles the Bald by name Judith. Baldwin Iron Arm begat Baldwin the Bald, who married

the daughter of King Edger of the English, by name Elftruda."[39]
Nor are these royal marriages the last enumerated by the anonymous author: Arnulf II (965–88) married Rozela Susanne,
daughter of King Berengar of Lombardy, and Baldwin V (1037–
67) married Adela, daughter of King Robert II of France. However, none of these royal unions is particularly favored or emphasized. It is rather the cumulative effect of these brilliant marriages that carries forward the comital family.

Around 1120, Lambert of Saint Omer included in his encyclo-
pedic compendium, the *Liber Floridus*, a genealogy of the counts
of Flanders that expanded on the received tradition and reincor-
porated information on Judith from the *Annals of St. Bertin*. In
his account, in 792, during the reign of Charlemagne, Lidricus,
the count of Harlebeke, found the region of Flanders deserted
and occupied it. Lambert then writes that Lidricus begat Ingelram, and Ingelram in turn begat Audricus/Audacer, the father
of Baldwin I "Ferreus." He then continues:

> Baldwin begat Baldwin the Bald from Judith, the widow of
> Adelbald king of the Angles, the daughter of Charles the Bald,
> king of the Franks. He [Adelbald] however died before taking
> her away as wife in the same year that he had accepted her.
> After his death, Judith, selling her possessions that she had
> obtained in the kingdom of the English, returned to her
> father and was being watched over under paternal guardian-
> ship at Senlis.[40]

Lambert then goes on to cite the story of her flight and marriage
to Baldwin in a verbatim citation from *the Annals of St. Bertin*,
as well as the story of the seduction, the excommunication of
the couple, their appeal to Pope Nicholas, and his eventual reconciliation of the king to his daughter and Baldwin.

As in the St. Bertin genealogy, the marriage of Baldwin and
Judith is the first of a series of royal marriages uniting counts of
Flanders with royal families. Lambert retained the language of

the St. Bertin *Annals*, Judith is still active in the affair, but she is not part of the foundation legend of the family. Rather, her enticement by Baldwin is paralleled by the seizure, two generations earlier, of Flanders by Count Lidricus of Harlebeke. It is this mythical figure who, in seizing what he wants from under the nose of Charlemagne, prefigures the audacity of Baldwin Iron Arm who seizes Charlemagne's great-granddaughter from under the nose of her father.

A final, even more elaborate genealogical account of the Flemish counts was written sometime after 1160. This text, the *Flandria generosa*, expands still further on the account in Lambert. Here, however, the action is clear: "In the year 862 Baldwin Iron Arm abducted Judith, widow of Adelbald, king of the English and daughter of Charles the Bald, king of the Franks."[41] The remainder of the account is virtually the same as that in Lambert and thus in the *Annals*, but interpolations in an early manuscript emphasize the obvious point that the abduction is all about Baldwin: Judith is said to have loved the count greatly on account of his "*probitas*," which might ironically be translated "uprightness." The pope is said to have agreed to intervene upon meeting Baldwin and seeing that he was "a very handsome young man and upright."[42]

As in Lambert, the story told in *Flandria generosa* of Baldwin's audacious marriage is no longer about Judith and certainly not the foundation story of the family. It is but one in a series of remarkable successes by this family of audacious and successful counts, who before and after Baldwin Iron Arm display the virtues of their "true" beginning, those of Lidricus.

Baldwin was no doubt quite a capable figure: had he not have been, Judith and her brother would certainly have chosen someone else as husband. However, what we see in the story of Baldwin and Judith is how the initial recognition of the foundation of the comital family made possible by a royal marriage fades as the male members of the family before and after are used to demonstrate a tradition of royal marriages and audacious deeds. Judith is no longer, as she was in the tenth century, the beginning of the family. She is but one more Carolingian property seized by a bold member of the Flemish dynasty.

And yet, this progressive erasure of Judith is anything but a simple reflection of the progressive marginalization of Flemish countesses during the eleventh and twelfth centuries. Quite the opposite is true.[43] Even while Judith was being reduced to one more clever conquest, a series of powerful countesses were playing active and critical roles in the governance of the county. In the eleventh century, Richtilde, the widow of Count Baldwin VI, fought to protect the rights of her sons Arnulf and Baldwin from their half-brother Robert the Frisian. Robert II's powerful wife Clementia of Burgundy, sister of Pope Calixtus II, shared power in Flanders with her son Baldwin following Robert's death in 1111. Sybil of Anjou, the second wife of Count Thierry, helped bring her husband into the patronage of King Henry II of England and twice served as regent while Thierry was at the Crusades, before accompanying him to Jerusalem and entering the convent of Saint-Lazarus at Bethany. These three women were just some of the powerful countesses in Flanders, who numbered among the most active, and at times most problematic, figures in Flemish history. One might see the effacement of Judith in genealogical memory as a critical response to, rather than a reflection of, women and power in the county.

The fates of the two Judiths in dynastic memory demonstrates both the vital importance of women in weaving the generations of a family and the strict limits to these women's roles. Daughters of kings or wives of kings brought enormous prestige and the chance for honors and riches to their male kindred both in their lifetimes and beyond. Both the Welfs and the Flemish counts long cherished and cultivated stories of their illustrious ancestry and close relationship with the Carolingian dynasty cemented through their Judiths. And yet, as time passed, one senses a reticence to attribute this good fortune to these founding mothers.

Henry of the Golden Plow, far from obtaining honor from his wife, was tempted by her to cast the honor and liberty of his family aside and managed, only through his own cleverness, to triumph. Lidricus, the mythical ancestor of the counts of Flanders, likewise managed to acquire his vast lands from the Carolingians, not as dowry or favor but through trickery. And ultimately Baldwin Iron Arm managed, by seducing Judith, to obtain his relationship to the king in spite of the latter.

In the ninth-century texts, both Judiths were participants in the fates of their husbands, but this too disappeared across the generations. The Judiths, like other women whose marriages made and sustained these families, were less participants in the rise of their husbands' fortunes than they were archetypal booty—among the first possessions that their husbands would acquire. Such was certainly not a description of these women at the origins of these families, nor was it an accurate description of the women who came after them, but it was the way that those responsible for family memory wished that they were.

Just why men might wish that women were less prominent in the origins and identities of their kindreds can perhaps be glimpsed by considering the effects on gender balance in the most important genealogy in the West, that of the family of Jesus.

CHAPTER FOUR

Writing Women In:
Sacred Genealogy
and Gender

In the previous chapters, we saw how authorities and societies might be gendered as feminine and thereby condemned
as illegitimate; how women who exercised power could be written out of history by relegating such power relations to a prehis-
torical age, the age of the Amazons; or how founding female
figures in family memory could fade in significance across the
generations. I turn now to the opposite phenomenon: the substi-
tution of a woman for a man in the most important genealogy
of Christendom: that of Mary for Joseph. The process itself is
generally well known, but I would like to retrace some of its
salient moments from the first to the twelfth centuries in order
to reflect on the process by which in the most important family
in Christian history, a founding mother was substituted for a
founding father.

The significance of Mary in Christian tradition from the second century cannot be overestimated.[1] Her centrality and significance extends far beyond her role as mother. Her representation in religious art increasingly took on the attributes of exalted
status, as a queen, the Queen of Heaven. As the central figure,
along with her Son, in the Christian economy of salvation, her

status as *genetrix* was but one of the multiple facets of her significance in Christian devotion and history.

The rise of Mary's status, however, led to the almost total eclipse of Joseph, who was not only eliminated from the genealogy, but marginalized and debased in popular tradition. This phenomenon, not reversed until the Renaissance, raises important questions about the limitations of gendered genealogical speculation and the dangers to patriarchal ideology of writing women into family history.

Of course, Mary and Joseph were much, much more than simple models either of parents or of husband and wife—the image of the "holy family" was a phenomenon of the Catholic reformation rather than the Middle Ages. Nor should the rise of Mary's status be seen as accompanying the rise in status of women in general: the dynamics of the cult of Mary certainly did not either reflect or parallel social values and norms in European society any more than Joseph's marginal status represented the position of men in this society. And yet the places of both in the genealogy of Jesus was fundamental, and fundamentally unequal.

Joseph, in contrast to his spouse, began and remained firmly fixed within the context of the nativity and childhood narratives of Jesus and Mary. What apocryphal and hagiographical traditions developed around him were entirely dependent on his place in the representations of Mary and Jesus. Although from the twelfth century there was a concerted effort to revalue Joseph as the *nutritor* (foster-father or nurturer of Jesus and Mary) or even as a model of patriarchal authority, this effort never succeeded in popular devotion before the fifteenth century.[2] Even the images of Joseph as nourisher and protector of the holy family developed in the iconography of gothic miniature painting could be reread or misread as evidence that he was a peasant, a boor, a low-born servant. This marginalization has wider implications for the general subject of women at the beginning because it suggests, at an implicit level, the problem of male authority in a family that drew its identity, status, and authority from a woman. Joseph ought to have had a central place in the holy family and in the story of the incarnation and redemption. From the twelfth century onward, theologians such as Bernard of Clairvaux attempted to buttress this position, to assert that Joseph too was central to the plan of salvation.[3] However, when we examine the tradition of genealogical speculation about the family of Jesus, the opposite is the case. In Western tradition, Joseph is progressively eliminated not only from paternity of Jesus but indeed from any paternity.

One might begin at the end, with the *Virga Jesse*, or Tree of Jesse, which appears from the end of the eleventh century as a visual representation of the descent of Jesus from King David, son of Jesse.[4] There was never a fixed format for the tree: it might include as few as four or as many as fifteen persons between Jesse and Jesus. Most were kings, with the primary figures almost invariably Jesse, David, Mary, and Jesus.[5] Joseph, the figure who in the Gospels is the guarantee of descent from Jesse, never appears as a link in the descent from David to Jesus. Normally, he is not present at all. An exception is the mid-twelfth-century Jesse Tree from Canterbury now in the Pierpont Morgan Library. But even here, he is not part of the genealogical tree but rather is present in a scene inserted into branches of the tree and is depicted in the marriage of the Virgin in the Roman ceremony of the contractual joining of the right hands by bride and groom before witnesses.[6]

Mary, not Joseph, is the figure who always guarantees the continuity from Jesse to David to Jesus. Although great variations in the iconography of the Tree of Jesse provided an ideal space for visual representation of the complexities of physical and spiritual kinship, the position of the Virgin is key, corresponding, in the words of Anita Guerreau-Jalabert, "to a pivot, the hinge around which is effected the passage from one form of parentage to the other."[7] Mary's position in Christian genealogy is indeed pivotal, but it is also nonscriptural and ambiguous—the weakest link in Christian reflection on Jesus's identity. It is also an erasure of the scriptural link between Jesus and David, Joseph.

Mary's insertion into Jesus's genealogy also contradicts a fundamental tenant of patriarchal identity formation. As the *Glossa ordinaria* states, "It is not the custom of the Scriptures that the order of women should be woven into generations."[8] And yet this is exactly what generations of Christian intellectuals have attempted to do. The result has been, on the one hand, a constant effort by ecclesiastics to transform how Western societies conceive of kinship and descent, and on the other, a constant if rarely stated tension between this ecclesiastical model of descent and an older, still potent emphasis on male generation and kinship.

Jesus's Davidic descent is vital to the Christian understanding of salvation and to Christian interpretation of Jewish scripture. However, Christian scripture is internally contradictory and raises ultimately insoluble problems concerning Jesus's parentage, ancestry, kindred, and the significance of Mary in these essential claims to this Davidic identity. In a nutshell the problem is this: Jesus's Davidic origins are based entirely on the genealogies in the Gospels of Matthew and Luke. These two genealogies contradict each other. More significantly, both of these genealogies are of Joseph, not of Mary. If Joseph was the legitimate father of Jesus, then there is no problem of his Davidic descent, but then he is not of divine origin; if Joseph was not his father, then the claim that he was of Davidic descent remains without foundation. Centuries of apologists and exegetes sought to resolve the paradox of how to place Mary as the only human parent of Jesus and yet preserve his descent from David.

Actually, this ought not to be a problem. Exegetes are quick to point out that biological descent was not the primary concern of either of the evangelists. Neither is concerned with biological continuity so much as legal continuity, a descent that within second temple Judaism could only be traced through the male line. These genealogies, as in the case of genealogies in general, are not about the past so much as about the present: they are arguments to establish identity, undergird status, and authenticate an office or function. Matthew was primarily concerned to show that Jesus was the son of David; Luke was concerned to show that he was the Son of God. Neither was particularly concerned either with the biological descent of Jesus from David or with the historical details of his genealogy.[9]

Patristic and medieval theologians were similarly concerned primarily with the spiritual and legal aspects of Jesus's Davidic descent. Rupert of Deutz, for example, focuses not on Jesus's biology but on his figurative descent from David through Joseph. Commenting on Jacob's ladder, which he interprets as the genealogy of Jesus, he writes:

> The highest rung of the ladder, by which the Lord is supported, is this blessed Joseph, husband of Mary, from whom Jesus who is called the Christ was born. In what manner was God and Lord supported by him? In the same way that a pupil depends on his tutor, in as much as he was born in this world without a father, thus he was supported by this blessed Joseph, that he should be the best father for this infant, that by his paternal solicitude the child along with his Virgin mother might be comforted.[10]

And yet, while theologians and exegetes might argue that something so prosaic as biological descent should not have been an issue, it most emphatically was. Genealogies may be about the present and the future; spiritual descent may be more significant than biological. Nevertheless from the first century, questions about Jesus's biological parentage created problems for Jesus's followers. The debate was not simply between his followers and skeptics but among the former—between those who sought to anchor their authority in their kinship with him and those who sought to undermine any claims to precedence based on kinship. On the one hand, apparently even during his lifetime, questions were raised about Jesus's legitimacy. Comments in the Gospel of Mark (6:3) and John (8:41) may suggest that Jesus was accused of illegitimacy by some of his opponents. In the century following his death, a tradition circulated that Jesus had been illegitimate. This may be echoed in Simeon ben Azzai who is said to have found in Jerusalem a genealogy dated to before the destruction of the Temple in which was written "So-and so is a *mamzer* [anyone born of relations between whom marriage is forbidden by the Mosaic law; a bastard] by a married woman."[11] The fullest version of this accusation is repeated in Origen's *Contra Celsum*, in which the third-century theologian quotes the second-century Celsus (writing in the persona of a Jew): "The mother of Jesus . . . having been turned out by the carpenter who was betrothed to her, as she had been convicted of adultery and had a child by a certain soldier named Panther."[12]

The responses from Jesus's followers to these accusations varied. Some emphasized that Jesus was indeed the legitimate son of Joseph and Mary; others insisted that Jesus was not illegitimate but nevertheless the son of the Virgin Mary who conceived through the power of the Holy Spirit. Among the former were Jewish followers of Jesus for whom Jesus's relationship to Joseph was essential for establishing his legitimacy and hence their authority. These included the Ebionites, Jewish followers of Christ from the Transjordanian area. "The Gospel of Nicodemus," or "Acts of Pilate," associated with this group, explicitly rejects allegations of Jesus's illegitimacy by emphasizing that his parents were legally married.[13] In an interrogation by Pilate, the witnesses to the betrothal of Joseph and Mary insist, in contradiction of the accusations of Annas and Caiaphas, that they are indeed Jews by birth, not converts, and that they were present at the betrothal of Joseph and Mary.[14]

Perhaps related to the Ebionites were those members of Joseph's family in Jerusalem who dominated the local Jesus community into the late first century. Jesus's paternity was crucial to this group because they drew their authority from their descent from Joseph's family; if Joseph were not actually related to Jesus, then their claims would be nullified. The third-century historian Eusebius reports, following a certain Heggesippus, a Jewish Christian who reported early traditions from Jerusalem, that Clopas, mentioned in John 19:25 and perhaps in Luke 24:18, had been a brother of Joseph and father of Symeon. After the death of James, Symeon succeeded his cousin because of his close relationship to Jesus. Obviously, if Jesus had not been the son of Joseph, Symeon's claims to the succession would have been greatly lessened.[15] As late as the 80s, according to Heggesippus, descendants of Clopas through Jesus's brother Jude continued to play a leading role among the Jewish followers of Jesus. So-called *Desposyni* (the Master's People), that is, the descendants of Jesus's family from Nazareth and Cochaba, Heggesippus further related, traveled about promoting such genealogical connections, presumably as part of a claim to authority within the movement. Since these are exactly the regions in which the Ebionites were reported to be active, one can perhaps see a direct relationship between this Jewish sect and the *Desposyni*.[16]

Claims to descend from the family of Jesus and Joseph might have produced a Christian kindred parallel to the Muslim Hashimids, who claim authority based on their descent from the Prophet.[17] However, the Roman persecution of the Davidites under Domitian in the 80s, along with the alternative Christian position that Jesus was no kin of Joseph, whether intentionally or not, helped to undermine this clan's prominence, particularly in non-Jewish Christian communities that comprised the vast majority of converts.

Henceforth, Joseph would largely disappear from Christian focus in favor of Mary, but this disappearing act had not been completed at the time that the evangelists were creating their genealogies of Jesus, each of which is actually a genealogy of Joseph. As a result, long after the descendants of Joseph had been forgotten, Christian apologists had to struggle to preserve the accuracy of scripture and the Davidic identity of Mary.

The two genealogies of Jesus that appear in the Gospels, one in the first chapter of Matthew and one in Luke 3:23–38, support the alternative Christian interpretation of Jesus's birth: he was the son of a virgin.[18] Both Gospels are at pains to emphasize that Jesus was the son of Mary and not of Joseph: "Joseph the husband of Mary, of whom Jesus was born, who is called Christ" (Matt. 1:16);[19] "Jesus . . . being the son (as was supposed) of Joseph" (Luke 3:23). Whether or not this emphasis on the virgin birth emerged in any way as an attempt by the opponents of the *Desposyni* to counter their claims to authority in the generations following Jesus's death, these three texts present fundamental problems: first, they remain genealogies of Joseph, not of Mary, even though Joseph was rapidly becoming irrelevant to the history of salvation. Second, they are not in agreement with each other: already the grandfather in Luke is named Heli, while Matthew calls him Jacob. Moreover, even at the crucial generation of David, Matthew's Jesus is the descendant of Solomon while Luke's descends from Nathan. How then was Jesus Davidic? The question clearly bothered Christians for centuries, and their solutions take us into a long and fascinating history of rationalizations and projections that profoundly influenced whole spheres of European thought.

An early attempt to reconcile the two genealogies was offered by Julius Africanus, an early third-century author who produced the first known attempt by a Christian to reconcile biblical and secular history and chronology. In a letter to one Aristides reproduced in part by Eusebius,[20] he proposed to reconcile the two genealogies by recourse to Levitical law.[21] Recalling the obligation of a man to father a child in the name of a brother who had died childless, he argued that the discrepancies in the genealogies present two different representations of Joseph's descent, one reckoned by nature, one by law:

> For the two families, descended from Solomon and Nathan respectively, were so interlocked by the re-marriage of childless widows and the "raising up" of offspring, that the same persons could rightly be regarded at different times as the children of different parents—sometimes the reputed fathers, sometimes the real.[22]

His proposed solution is that Luke provides the legal genealogy and Matthew the biological genealogy. He presents the genealogies as follows (apparently working with a manuscript of Luke that omits two generations):

Luke	Matthew
Melchi	Matthan
Heli	Jacob
Joseph	Joseph

Melchi and Matthan were from different families but were successive husbands of the same wife and fathered half-brothers. This wife, Estha, first married Matthan, the descendant of Solomon, and bore him Jacob. Then, on the death of Matthan, she married Melchi, of the family of Nathan, and bore Heli. In the next generation, Heli died childless, and his brother Jacob took his wife and by her became the father of Joseph. Thus, according to nature, Joseph was his son, but according to law, Joseph was the son of Heli. This rather complex argumentation, which Africanus says was preserved among the *Desposyni*, offered a possible reconciliation of the two genealogies (although the two omitted generations in that of Luke, Levi and Matthat, present further problems). However, this solution does not deal with the relationship of Mary to David, an issue of no importance to the

Desposyni, who apparently traced their descent from Joseph, but one of fundamental significance to later generations. Eusebius attempts to finesse this problem:

> In tracing thus the genealogy of Joseph, Africanus has virtually proved that Mary belonged to the same tribe as her husband, in view of the fact that under the Mosaic law intermarriage between different tribes was forbidden, for the rule is that a woman must wed someone from the same town and the same clan, so that the family inheritance may not be moved from tribe to tribe.[23]

Although this solution did not satisfy everyone in subsequent generations it did provide a popular solution to the dilemma that would be incorporated into the *Glossa ordinaria*.[24]

As the significance of Mary grew to the detriment of Joseph, she was provided first with an immediate family and then with a genealogy connecting her more explicitly to the house of David. The earliest recorded conjectures that provided Mary with parents appears in the *Protoevangelium of James*, a Greek work written sometime around the middle of the second century by a Christian from either Syria or Egypt.[25] The *Protoevangelium* answers questions unanswered in the canonical Gospels. For our purposes, the *Protoevangelium* answers three important questions about Mary's ancestry and kindred. First, it provides her with parents, Anna and Joachim, the former clearly modeled on Hannah, mother of Samuel, and the latter on the long tradition of biblical figures beginning with Abraham who were without offspring until the Lord showed mercy on them. Second, it explains the conception of Mary, which took place through the miraculous intervention of an angel. Third, it explains the references to "brothers of the Lord" by stating that Joseph was an old man when he was betrothed to Mary and had children by a previous marriage.

The *Protoevangelium* had great success in the Greek-speaking world where the cult of Anna was well established by the fourth century. In the West, following the objections of Jerome to such apocrypha,[26] outside of Rome with its large populations of Greek-speaking Christians, Anna and Joachim reached the Latin-speaking world only slowly, and by a circuitous route.

While the Latin orthodox church of the fifth and sixth centuries largely ignored the apocryphal tradition of Mary, North African Donatists, with their strong emphasis on legitimate succession, were both fascinated with such genealogies and under no compunctions about incorporating the *Protoevangelium* into their tradition. Sometime around 390, a North African, possibly one Q. Julius Hilarianus, wrote a short treatise that sought to combine and reconcile all of the biblical genealogies. Although the question of whether the original version of this text was Donatist is in dispute, it very quickly was absorbed into a Donatist tradition that long survived the Vandal conquest of North Africa. In composing this *Origo humani generis*, Hilarianus draws almost entirely on scripture, using a version of the pre-Jerome Latin Bible and some of the apocrypha such as the third book of Esdras.[27] His work culminates with the birth of Jesus, first recounting the genealogy in Matthew, ending with Joseph: "Jacob begat Joseph, that is, coming together, of whom, as it was thought Christ the Lord was the son according to the flesh."[28]

But he then turns to the genealogy in Luke: "Let us return to Nathan brother of Salomon from whom Mary takes her origin." This time he follows the genealogy in Luke with a few omissions coming at last to Joseph. However, this is a different Joseph:

> Joseph begat Ioachim. Ioachim begat mother Mary mother of the lord Jesus Christ. Luke introduces this descent from Nathan and Matthew that from Salomon so that one might know that from the root of Jesse, that is from David, descended both Joseph and Mother Mary.[29]

This bold but simple solution, namely of ascribing the Lucan genealogy to Mary and making the Joseph in this genealogy Mary's grandfather, was preserved in the Donatist communities of North Africa and ultimately crossed the Strait of Gibraltar and took root in Visigothic Spain. There it was incorporated into the elaborate genealogies that appear in the manuscripts of the Beatus commentary on the *Apocalypse*, itself probably based on late Roman African exemplars, and thus entered European circulation.[30]

Elsewhere, however, the idea of making Joseph Mary's own grandfather did not find resonance. However, an alternative version of how the Lucan genealogy could become that of Mary was offered by John of Damascus (ca. 676–787), who likewise saw Luke's genealogy as that of Mary, but astonishingly added to this genealogy the name of the very Panther who had been in some Jewish traditions identified as the Roman soldier who was the father of Jesus. "Thus from the chain of Nathan son of David, Levi begat Melchi and Panther; Panther begat Barpanther. This Barpanther begat Ioachim. Ioachim begat the holy mother of God."[31] This tradition entered the Latin West in the mid-twelfth century through Burgundo of Pisa, was incorporated into texts as widely diffused as Jacobus de Voragine's *Golden Legend*, and became an alternative means of Mary rather than Joseph being the bearer of Jesus's Davidic heritage.[32]

Along with the moves to eliminate Joseph from the genealogy of Jesus were moves to make those identified in the Gospels as Jesus's kin related to him through his mother's family rather than through that of Joseph. As we have seen in Eusebius, Clopias, father of Symeon, was the brother of Joseph. The *Protoevangelium* supports the tradition that Jesus's "brothers" were sons of Joseph by a previous marriage. However, by the fifth century, Jerome was insisting that the "brethren" of the Lord were his relatives through his mother.[33] In the form of the Gospel of Pseudo-Matthew, a text of probably the eighth or ninth century based largely on the *Protoevangelium* but accompanied by a forged letter of Jerome testifying to its veracity, the Anna and Joachim tradition took root in the West.[34] However, although Pseudo-Matthew makes James, Joseph, Judah, and Simeon sons of Joseph by a previous marriage, this aspect of the story did not dominate in the West. After some tentative formulations, in the mid-ninth century, Haymo of Auxerre resolved the complexities of the relationships within the Gospel by arguing that not only were the brothers of the Lord sons of his mother's sisters, but that these sisters were the three Marys, each a daughter of Anna by a different father. Drawing on the Pseudo-Matthew, available for less than a century with its forged authentication by pseudo-Jerome, he offers the following solution.

First Anna married Joachim, and from him gave birth to Mary the mother of the Lord. After Joachim had died, she married Cleopha, and from him had the other Mary, who is called in the Gospels Maria Clephae. Moreover, Cleopha had a brother Joseph, to whom he affianced his stepdaughter, the blessed Mary. He gave his actual daughter to Alpheo, from whom was born James the Lesser who is also called Justus, brother of the Lord, and the other Joseph. After Cleopha died, Anna married a third husband, Salome, and had from him the third Mary, from whom, after being married to Zebadae, were born James the Greater and the evangelist John.[35] This invention of the three husbands of Anna eliminated the last role of Joseph: the father of the "brethren" of Jesus.

The progressive elimination of a significant role for Joseph in the kindred of Jesus is paralleled by the increasing divergence in representation of Joseph in iconography. The iconography of Joseph from the fourth century to the thirteenth remains quite limited. He has no independent iconographic tradition apart from the holy family: he is represented dreaming one of the three dreams in Luke's Gospel, and he is present at the engagement with Mary, at the journey to Bethlehem, the Nativity, the

Adoration of the Magi, and in some scenes from the *Proto-evangelium*—the trial by bitter water of Mary and the so-called episode of Afrodisius, when temple idols fall at the arrival of Jesus in Egypt.[36]

In the earliest representations, such as fourth-century representations of the Magi, Joseph stands behind a chair in which is seated Mary holding the Christ child. The representations of Joseph and Mary are in a realistic style, and Joseph, standing beside Mary, is the image of a paterfamilias. As Paolo Testini has suggested, however, the relative equality with which Mary and Joseph are treated in such early works changes progressively in the fifth century, a change he attributes reasonably to the Council of Ephesus and the elevation of Mary as Theotokos and queen of virgins.[37] Mary increasingly carries the attributes of a queen or woman of power and splendor. Not so her husband, whose representation maintains its original simplicity, if he is not devalued either in size, in height in the image, or in physical appearance. His age, emphasized in the *Protoevangelium* and the Pseudo-Matthew, increases as does his infirmity. Generally, if not absolutely consistently, in subsequent representations he appears not so much her protector as her servant.

The attempts to revalue Joseph beginning in the twelfth century seem, in spite of Bernard of Clairvaux, Rupert of Deutz, and later Franciscan and Dominican preachers, to have met with extraordinarily limited success.[38] There are virtually no church dedications to Joseph from the Middle Ages;[39] no hagiographical tradition develops apart from the apocryphal traditions of the infancy narratives. When, at the end of the fourteenth century, Jean Gerson attempted to develop a cult of Joseph as a model of patriarchial authority, his efforts met with total failure.[40] Even the symbolic representations of Joseph as the nutritor of the holy family failed to convey consistently the message that such symbols of nurturing intended. Images of Joseph as cook, for example, however well intended, became the material of ridicule.[41]

The representation of Joseph and the flight into Egypt could be read, by the fifteenth century, as old, spent, broken, a fool.

What does all this tell us about the elaboration of a Christian origin legend and the place of Mary within it? First, the stages of transformation and elaboration of these legends are radically discontinuous: the early conflicts between the kin of Jesus and other Christians were quickly forgotten, even by the time of Eusebius, who nevertheless recorded their echoes in the form of the information on the *Desposyni*. Donatist concerns with descent and genealogy provided a fertile ground for the reception of genealogical elaborations, but by the time they reached Europe and were incorporated into the Beatus tradition, their relationship to the persecuted and proscribed sect were forgotten. Carolingian incorporation of apocrypha depended on the creation of a forged letter of Jerome that presumably gave authority to the very texts the actual Jerome had condemned. By the twelfth century, when Damascene tradition was being widely diffused, nothing of the prehistories of Panther were known in the West. And yet all of this miscellaneous and contradictory material was reworked and recombined as fundamental elements of the Marian tradition.

Second, the instability of the tradition testifies to the inadequacy of any of these attempts to reconcile all of the scriptural and traditional details. Just as there was never a definitive version of the Tree of Jesse, there was never a definitive resolution of the relationship between the genealogies of Matthew and Luke. Mary's kindred remained open-ended, with Anna as the matriarch of a diffuse family of saints and apostles.

Finally, as Mary assumed the biological role of providing Jesus with Davidic identity, Joseph lost not only his position within Christian salvation history but his dignity as well. Here I believe is reflected in a negative manner the danger presented if "the order of women should be woven into generations": the order of men loses both authority and dignity. By the fourteenth century,

Gerson could attempt to promote the cult of Joseph, to emphasize that as father of the holy family he commanded both Mary
and Jesus, but such exhortations fell on deaf ears. Mary's relationship to Jesus and the Davidic promise may always have been
spiritual and symbolic, but it was also understood as carnal. In
a family in which a woman played this role, even if she was the
Virgin Mary, her husband could be nothing but an object of
scorn. This was a lesson that even the most enlightened and de-
voted father and husband could not but recognize.

Women at the End

The two Judiths, like Libuše, the mother of the Bohemian ducal family, and Gambara, the mother of the Lombards, like the Amazons among the Goths, were there at the beginning of their respective peoples, but not at the end. While foundational texts may have given such characters central roles for reasons of female patronage or ideology, over time they fail in male discourse as exemplars of social structure and political power. By the twelfth century, the Judiths are passive conquests of their dynamic husbands, evidence of the glory of their husbands' kindred but not in any sense its cause. Libuše too fades from the scene, and with her the type of woman she represented: "After the death of Princess Libuše, our women are subject to the authority of men," wrote Cosmas. Similarly, after the wise and protective Gambara, came the mother of Lamissio, an unnamed prostitute, "more cruel than all wild beasts." Fittingly, when the Lombards were barred from crossing a river by the Amazons, Lamissio himself swam into the river, killed the most powerful of the Amazons, and won passage for his people.[1] Good or evil, wise or foolish, women cede to men, Amazons are defeated by warriors, and the proper order is returned to the world.

But there is Mary. Within the Western Christian tradition, one woman retains her place at the beginning and at the end.

She, along with her mother Anna, are at the center of a different family, the sacred family, that draws its identity unambiguously from these two exceptional women. Anna is the dowager mother, the thrice widowed woman who, through her daughters, stands at the center of the family of the apostles. And Mary herself stands at the center of salvation. She accomplishes what the Judith of the Hebrew Bible or those of the Carolingians could not: to remain at the end as well as the beginning.

But as we have seen, such success comes at a price. For all the possible multiplicities of origins, the medieval idolatry of origins seems curiously monotheistic: there is room for a man or a woman, but not both. Conceptualizing family as a social group in which men stand at the center cannot but diminish the women, and conversely women who stand in the center cannot but diminish the men.

Of course, the progressive effacement of Gambara, Libuše, or the Judiths is not reflective of the complex possibilities of real women in the worlds in which these texts were written or reworked. By the same token, the rise of Mary is hardly evidence of the rise of women's access to power and autonomy at the expense of men in the first centuries of the second millennium. All of these figures have their existences within textual and narrative worlds that intersect the world of lived experience in complex and often paradoxical ways.

And yet, in contrast to the modeling of origins in antiquity, powerful, autonomous women were at least thinkable in medieval Europe. In a spirituality elaborated by an increasingly celibate clergy and directed toward the patronage of powerful women, thinking of women at the center, with all of its troubling and subversive implications, grew as a spiritual model of social organization and legitimacy. It would be centuries before Joseph finally became a popular object of male piety, just as it would be centuries before families and kingdoms could be headed by women who, neither widows nor guardian mothers, ruled as well as reigned. Still, within the contradictory ways that the past was used to understand the present and future, that origins were seen as destinations, some room had appeared in the mental landscape for women who not only began but endured and prevailed.

Notes

ACKNOWLEDGMENTS

1. *The Myth of Nations: The Medieval Origins of Europe* (Princeton, NJ: Princeton University Press, 2002).

2. Patrick Geary, "Cur in feminas tamdiu perseverat?" in Walter Pohl, ed., *Die Suche nach den Ursprüngen: Von der Bedeutung des Frühen Mittelalters,* Forschungen zur Geschichte des Mittelalters 8 (Vienna: Verlag der Österreichischen Akademie der Wissenschaft, 2004), pp. 37–44.

INTRODUCTION

1. Genesis 3:6.

2. Herodotus, 4.9.

3. Jordanes, *Getica*, 7.49 ed. Theodor Mommsen, Monumenta Germaniae Historica (hereafter MGH) Auctores antiquissimi (hereafter AA) 5 (Berlin, 1882), p. 67.

4. Paulus Diaconus, *Historia Langobardorum*, 1.8, ed. Georg Waitz, MGH Scriptores rerum Germanicarum in usum scholarum (hereafter SSRG i.u.s.) 48 (Hanover, 1878), p. 58.

5. Cosmas of Prague, *Chronica Boemorum*, 1.4, Cosmas von Prag, *Die Chronik der Böhmen*, ed. B. Bretholz, MGH Scriptores rerum Germanicarum, Nova series 2 (Berlin, 1923), p. 11.

6. Witger, *Genealogia Arnulfi Comitis*, ed. L. C. Bethmann, MGH Scriptores (in Folio)(hereafter SS) 9 (Hanover, 1851), p. 303.

7. *Liber genealogus*, ed. Theodor Mommsen, MGH AA 9, *Chronica Minora saec IV.V.VI.VII* (Munich, 1981), p. 194.

8. Reuven Firestone, *Journeys in Holy Lands: The Evolution of the Abraham-Ishmael Legends in Islamic Exegesis* (Albany: State University of New York Press, 1990), pp. 63–71.

9. Widukind, *Rerum gestarum saxonicarum*, ed. Paul Hirsch and Hans-Eberhard Lohmann, MGH SSRG i.u.s. 60 (Hanover, 1882), 1.9, pp. 6–10.

10. Paulus Diaconus, 2.28.

11. Cosmas of Prague, 1. 3–4, pp. 7–13.

12. Who first appears in the medieval *Alfabeta de-Ben Sira*, ed. Moritz Steinschneider (Berlin: Bi-defus Fridlender, 1858). See Maaike van der Lugt, "Pourquoi Dieu a-t-il créé la femme? Différence sexuelle et théologie médiévale," in Jean-Claude Schmitt, ed., *Ève et Pandora: La création de la femme* (Paris: Gallimard, 2001), pp. 89–113, esp. 92–95.

13. Jordanes, *Getica*, 24, p. 89.

14. Gregory of Tours, *Historiarum libri X*, 2.28–31, ed. Bruno Krusch and Wilhelm Levison, MGH Scriptores rerum Merovingicarum (hereafter SSRM) 1 (Hanover, 1951), pp. 89–93 for 2.28–31.

15. Widukind, 3.66–68.

16. Jo Ann McNamara, "*Imitatio Helenae*: Sainthood as an Attribute of Queenship," in Sandro Sticca, ed., *Saints: Studies in Hagiography* (Binghamton: Center for Medieval and Renaissance Studies, State University of New York, 1996), pp. 51–80.

17. On Melusine, see Claude Lecouteux, *Mélusine et le Chevalier au cygne* (Paris: Imago, 1997); Donald Maddox and Sara Sturm-Maddox, *Melusine of Lusignan: Founding Fiction in Late Medieval France* (Athens: University of Georgia Press, 1996); and Jeanne-Marie Boivin and Proinsias MacCana, eds., *Mélusines continentales et insulaires*, Actes du colloque international tenu les 27 et 28 mars 1997 à l'Université Paris XII et au Collège des Irlandais (Paris: Honoré Champion Editeur, 1999).

18. Jean-Claude Schmitt, ed., *Ève et Pandora*, Introduction, p. 22.

19. Especially in his *Women of the Twelfth Century*, trans. Jean Birrell, 3 vols. (Chicago: University of Chicago Press, 1998).

20. See in particular the essays in Theodore Evergates, ed., *Aristocratic Women in Medieval France* (Philadelphia: University of Pennsylvania Press, 1999), esp. Amy Livingstone, "Aristocratic Women in the Chartrain," pp. 44–73, esp. 46–47; and Theodore Evergates, "Aristocratic Women in the Country of Champagne," pp. 74–110, who concludes: "The evidence from Champagne is ample and unambiguous. If historians have missed the pervasive presence of women in aristocratic society it is because they have made unwarranted assumptions about the organization of families and the descent of property" (110). Constance Brittain Bouchard, *Those of My Blood: Constructing Noble*

Families in Medieval Francia (Philadelphia: University of Pennsylvania Press, 2001); and the discussion by Jo Ann McNamara, "Women and Power through the Family Revisited," in Mary C. Erler and Maryanne Kowaleski, eds., *Gendering the Master Narrative: Women and Power in the Middle Ages* (Ithaca, NY: Cornell University Press, 2003), pp. 17–30, esp. 20–22.

CHAPTER ONE

1. Marc Bloch, *The Historian's Craft*, trans. Peter Putnam (New York: Alfred A. Knopf, 1953), pp. 29–35.

2. Ibid., p. 30.

3. Perhaps the most influential author on primitive matriarchy was Marija Gimbutas. See in particular her *The Civilization of the Goddess: The World of Old Europe* (San Francisco: Harper San Francisco, 1991). For a summary of the issues, see Merry E. Wiesner-Hanks, *Gender in History* (Oxford: Blackwell Publishers, 2001), esp. pp. 14–18.

4. For a thorough critique of this approach, see Cynthia Eller, *The Myth of Matriarchal Prehistory: Why an Invented Past Won't Give Women a Future* (Boston: Beacon Press, 2000).

5. Walter Pohl, "Gender and Ethnicity in the Early Middle Ages," in Leslie Brubaker and Julia M. H. Smith, eds., *Gender in the Early Medieval World: East and West, 300–900* (Cambridge: Cambridge University Press, 2004), pp. 23–43, esp. 30–32.

6. See below, chapter 2, pp. 27–28 on the archaeological evidence of women warriors. The question of archaeological evidence of warrior women is part of a larger problem of gender in archaeology, an issue only recently coming into prominence. See the essays in Joan M. Gero and Margaret W. Conkey, eds., *Engendering Archaeology: Women and Prehistory* (Oxford: Basil Blackwell, 1991); Rita P. Wright, ed., *Gender and Archaeology* (Philadelphia: University of Pennsylvania Press, 1996); and, for the early Middle Ages, in particular Guy Halsall, "Female Status and Power in Early Merovingian Central Austrasia: The Burial Evidence," *Early Medieval Europe* 5 (1996): 1–24. However, as Halsall concludes on p. 24, even if "gender is not a binary divide," it would be equally incorrect to assume that the early Middle Ages was some "golden age" for women, and certainly no Western medieval evidence points to the existence of warrior women.

7. *Chronicon Montis Sereni*, ed. E. Eherenfeuchter, MGH SS 23 (Hanover, 1874), p. 176. Cited by Robert Bartlett in "Reflections on Paganism and Chris-

tianity in Medieval Europe," *Proceedings of the British Academy* 101 (1998): 55–76, esp. 61.

8. Gert Melville, "L'institutionnalité médiévale dans sa pluridimensionnalité," in Jean-Claude Schmitt and Otto Gerhard Oexle, eds., *Les tendances actuelles de l'histoire du Moyen Age en France et en Allemagne* (Paris: Publications de la Sorbonne, 2003), p. 244. See further examples in Peter Wunderli, ed., *Herkunft und Ursprung: Historische und mythische Formen der Legitimation* (Sigmaringen: J. Thorbecke, 1994).

9. *Biblia Latina cum glossa ordinaria: Facsimile Reprint of the editio Princeps Adolph Rusch of Strassburg 1480/81,* introduction by Karlfried Froehlich and Margaret T. Gibson (Turnhout: Brepols, 1992), 4.6.

10. R. Howard Bloch, *Etymologies and Genealogies: A Literary Anthropology of the French Middle Ages* (Chicago: University of Chicago Press, 1983), p. 37.

11. Within the voluminous literature on women and gender in antiquity, see in particular the essays in Elaine Fantham et al., *Women in the Classical World: Image and Text* (New York: Oxford University Press, 1994), with the bibliographical suggestions following each essay.

12. Herodotus, 4.5–7.

13. François Hartog, *Le miroir d'Hérodote: Essai sur la représentation de l'autre* (Paris: Gallimard, 1991), esp. p. 43.

14. Hartog, *Le miroir,* pp. 44–46; Elias J. Bickerman, "*Origines Gentium,*" *Classical Philology* 47 (1952): 65–81; esp. 71–72.

15. "Ce rêve d'une hérédité purement paternelle n'a jamais cessé de hanter l'imagination grecque." Jean-Pierre Vernant, "Hestia-Hermès: Sur l'expression religieuse de l'espace et du mouvement chez les Grecs," in Jean-Pierre Vernant, *Mythe et pensée chez les Grecs: Étude de psychologie historique,* 2 vols. (Paris: Petite Collection Maspero, 1974), p. 106.

16. Nicole Loraux, *Les enfants d'Athéna: Idées athéniennes sur la citoyenneté et la division des sexes* (Paris: François Maspero, 1981).

17. On Pandora, see Jean-Pierre Vernant, "Pandora," in Jean-Claude Schmitt, ed. *Ève et Pandora,* pp. 29–66.

18. See in general Ralph Hexter, "Sidonian Dido," in Ralph Hexter and Daniel Selden, eds., *Innovations of Antiquity* (New York: Routledge, 1992), pp. 332–84.

19. On the multiple Didos of antiquity and the Middle Ages, see Christopher Baswell, "Dido's Purse," in Margaret Bridges, Guillemette Bolens, and Fabienne Michelet, eds., *Cultures in Contact, Past and Present: Studies in Honor of Paul Beekman Taylor,* special issue of *Multilingua* 18 (1999): 159–72, citation on 160.

20. Baswell, "Dido's Purse," pp. 166–69.

21. On the different ways that Roman historians restructured the story of Lucretia, see Melissa M. Matthes, *The Rape of Lucretia and the Founding of Republics: Readings in Livy, Machiavelli, and Rousseau* (University Park: Pennsylvania State University Press, 2000), esp. pp. 23–50; and Marie Theres Fögen, *Römische Rechtsgeschichten: Über Ursprung und Evolution eines sozialen Systems* (Göttingen: Vandenhoeck and Ruprecht, 2002), pp. 21–59.

22. Livy, 3.44–48, quotation from 3.48.

23. Fögen, *Römische Rechtsgeschichten*, pp. 61–124.

24. Hans-Werner Goetz, *Frauen im frühen Mittelalter* (Weimar: Böhlau, 1995), pp. 71–103.

25. Goetz, *Frauen*, p. 97, citing commentaries of Bede, Remigius of Auxerre, and Alcuin.

26. Although following Paul, not all commentators were prepared to see woman made in the image of God. See Laurent Angliviel de la Beaumelle, "Ève à l'épreuve des Pères," in Jean-Claude Schmitt, ed., *Ève et Pandora*, pp. 69–87, esp. 82–84.

27. "Esca illa [the forbidden fruit] mater mortis hominibus facta est." Joannes Scotus Erigena, *De divisione naturae*, 4.16, Patrologiae cursus completus . . . Series Latina (hereafter PL), ed. J.-P. Migne (Paris: J.-P. Migne, 1841–1902), 122:821, citing Gregory of Nissa.

28. On the tower of Babel in European tradition, see Arno Borst, *Der Turmbau von Babel: Geschichte der Meinungen über Ursprung und Vielfalt der Sprachen und Völker*, 4 vols. in 6 (Stuttgart: A. Hiersemann, 1957–63). See also the general reflections of František Graus, *Lebendige Vergangenheit: Überlieferung im Mittelalter und in den Vorstellungen vom Mittelalter* (Vienna: Böhlau, 1975).

29. See in particular Reuven Firestone, *Journeys in Holy Lands*; Andrew Rippin, "Sara," in C. E. Bosworth et al., eds., *The Encyclopaedia of Islam*, 2nd ed. (Leiden: E. J. Brill, 1995), 8:26–27.

30. On the complex question of Mary as model, see Hedwig Röckelein, Claudia Opitz, and Dieter R. Bauer, eds., *Maria Abbild oder Vorbild? Zur Sozialgeschichte mittelalterlicher Marienverehrung* (Tübingen: Edition Diskord, 1990), esp. Hedwig Röckelein and Claudia Opitz, "Für eine Sozialgeschichte mittelalterlicher Marienverehrung," pp. 11–18, for methodological reflections. On Mary in sacred genealogy see below, chapter 4.

31. Herwig Wolfram et al., "Origo gentis," in *Reallexikon der Germanischen Altertumskunde*, 2nd ed. (Berlin: de Gruyter, 2003), 22:174–83; and Pohl, "Gender and Ethnicity." From a different perspective, see Susan Reynolds, "Medieval *origines gentium* and the Community of the Realm," *History* 68 (1983): 375–390, and her "Our Forefathers? Tribes, Peoples, and Nations in the Historiogra-

phy of the Age of Migrations," in Alexander Callander Murray, ed., *After Rome's Fall: Narrators and Sources of Early Medieval History* (Toronto: University of Toronto Press, 1998), pp. 17–34.

32. The other *origo gentis* is the *origo gentis Romanae*. See Wolfram against Elias J. Bickerman, *"Origines gentium," Classical Philology* 47 (1952): 65–81. On the *Origo gentis Romanae*, see Arnaldo Momigliano, "Some Observations on the 'Origo gentis Romanae,' " *Journal of Roman Studies* 48 (1958): 56–73.

33. The approach is most closely associated with Walter Goffart, *The Narrators of Barbarian History (A.D. 550–800): Jordanes, Gregory of Tours, Bede and Paul the Deacon* (Princeton, NJ: Princeton University Press, 1988).

34. Pohl, "Gender and Ethnicity," p. 43.

35. On the politics of royal genealogies, see David Dumville, "Kingship, Genealogies and Regnal Lists," in Peter H. Sawyer and Ian N. Wood, eds., *Early Medieval Kingship* (Leeds: School of History, University of Leeds 1977), pp. 72–104. On the elaboration and myths of Anglo-Saxon origins, see Nicholas Howe, *Migration and Mythmaking in Anglo-Saxon England* (New Haven, CT: Yale University Press, 1989); and, in general, Ian N. Wood, "Anglo-Saxons," in Wolfram et al., *Origo Gentis,*" pp. 199–203.

36. See in particular Heide Estes, "Feasting with Holofernes: Digesting Judith in Anglo-Saxon England," *Exemplaria* 15 (2003): 325–50.

37. Jordanes, *Getica,* 24, p. 89.

38. Pohl, "Gender and Ethnicity," p. 37.

39. Paulus Diaconus, *Historia Langobardorum,* 3.35, pp. 140–41.

40. See Pohl, "Gender and Ethnicity," p. 38.

41. Walter Pohl, "Paolo Diacono e la costruzione dell'identità longobarda," in Paolo Chiesa, ed., *Paolo Diacono—uno scrittore fra tradizione longobarda e rinnovamento carolingio* (Udine: Forum, 2000), pp. 413–26.

42. Janet L. Nelson, "Perceptions du pouvoir chez les historiennes du haute moyen âge," in Michel Rouche and Jean Heuclin, eds., *La femme au moyen-âge* (Ville de Maubeuge: Diffusion Jean Touzot, 1990), pp. 75–83.

43. Lisa M. Bitel, *Women in Early Medieval Europe, 400–1100* (Cambridge: Cambridge University Press, 2002), 53.

Chapter Two

1. Jordanes, *Getica,* 7.49, p. 67.

2. Jordanes, *Getica,* 9, p. 70. "Sed ne dicas de viris Gothorum sermo adsumptus cur in feminas tamdiu perseverat?"

3. Cosmas of Prague, *Chronica Boemorum,* 1.9, p. 19.

4. Paulus Diaconus, *Historia Langobardorum*, 1.15, pp. 61–62.

5. Fredegar, *Chronicarum quae dicuntur Fredegarii Scholastici libri IV*, ed. Bruno Krusch, MGH SSRM 2 (Hanover, 1888) 2.4, p. 45; 2.62, p. 85.

6. Bede, In *Esdram et Nehemiam Allegorica expositio*, 2.10, PL 91:869.

7. Adam of Bremen, *Gesta Hammaburgensis ecclesiae pontificum*, ed. Bernhard Schmeidler, MGH SSRG i.u.s. 2 (Hanover, 1917; reprint, 1993), 3.16, p. 157 and 4.19, pp. 246–47.

8. Walter Goffart, *The Narrators of Barbarian History*. For example, "The occasions for amusement occur when Roman negligence awakens in the Goths the ancient—and humorous—Amazon strain" (pp. 80–81).

9. Pohl, "Gender and Ethnicity," p. 9.

10. See Bitel, *Women in Early Medieval Europe, 400–1100*, pp. 76–80.

11. Jeannine Davis-Kimball, *Warrior Women: An Archaeologist's Search for History's Hidden Heroines* (New York: Warner Books, 2002). Attempts to date such women's tombs to the periods when Amazons are reported, however, remain elusive.

12. On the literature, see Walter Pohl, *Die Awaren: Ein Steppenvolk in Mitteleuropa 567–822 n.Ch.* (Munich: Verlag C. H. Beck, 1988), p. 306.

13. Pohl, "Gender and Ethnicity," pp. 24–36.

14. On Jordanes's use of the *Historia Augusta*, see Jacques Schwartz, "Jordanès et l'Histoire Auguste," *Bonner Historia-Augusta-Colloquium 1979/81*, *Antiquitas Reihe* 4, 15 (Bonn, 1983), pp. 275–84. Schwartz believes that Jordanes probably knew the *Historia Augusta* indirectly through Symmiacs or Cassidorus. On the appearance of Gothic Amazons in the *Historia Augusta*, see Herwig Wolfram, *History of the Goths*, trans. Thomas J. Dunlap (Berkeley: University of California Press, 1988), p. 28 and n. 87. Also Pohl, "Gender and Ethnicity."

15. Reinhold Bichler, "Herodots Frauenbild und seine Vorstellung über die Sexualsitten der Völker," in Robert Rollinger and Christoph Ulf, eds., *Geschlechterrollen und Frauenbild in der Perspektive antiker Autoren* (Innsbruck: Studien Verlag, 2000), pp. 13–56, esp. 31.

16. *Historia Augusta* (from *Divus Aurelianus*, vol. 3 of the Loeb edition, *The Scriptores historiae augustae*, trans. David Magie, 3 vols. [Cambridge, MA: Harvard University Press, 1960–61])(hereafter *HA*), 22.3.

17. "Ductae sunt et decem mulieres, quas virili habitu pugnantes inter Gothos ceperat, cum multae essent interemptae, quas de Amazonum genere titulus indicabat—praelati sunt tituli gentium nomina continents." *HA*, Aurelian, 34.1.

18. Michael McCormick, *Eternal Victory: Triumphal Rulership in Late Antiquity, Byzantium and the Early Medieval West* (Cambridge: Cambridge University Press, 1986), p. 14.

19. *HA* 13.3–5, pp. 43–45 (Vita Galieni); Richard Stoneman, *Palmyra and Its Empire: Zenobia's Revolt against Rome* (Ann Arbor: University of Michigan Press, 1992).

20. *HA*, Thirty Pretenders, 30.1., p. 135.

21. Edmond Frézouls, "Le rôle politique des femmes dans l'*Histoire auguste*," in Giorgio Bonamente and François Paschoud eds., *Historiae Augustae: Colloquium Genevense; Atti dei Convegni sulla Historia Augusta II* (Bari: Edipuglia, 1994), pp. 121–36, citation on p. 136. On Zenobia in the *HA*, see also J. F. Gilliam, "Three Passages in the *Historia Augusta*: Gord. 21.5 and 34, 2–6; Tyr. Trig. 30.12," *Bonner Historia-Augusta-Colloquium 1968–1969* (Bonn, 1970), pp. 99–110.

22. *Pompeius Trogus fragmenta*, ed. Otto Seel (Leipzig: Teubner, 1956). See also Justin, *Epitome of the Philippic History of Pompeius Trogus*, translation and appendixes by J. C. Yardley, commentary by Waldemar Heckel (Oxford: Clarendon Press, 1997).

23. Orosius, 7.40. See Hans-Werner Goetz, *Die Geschichtstheologie des Orosius*, Impulse der Forschung 32 (Darmstadt: Wissenschaftliche Buchgesellschaft, 1980), pp. 133–34.

24. Orosius, 1.16, trans. Irving Woodworth Raymond, *The Seven Books of History against the Pagans: The Apology of Paulus Orosius* (New York: Columbia University Press, 1936), p. 64. Hans-Werner Goetz does not discuss Orosius's Amazons in his *Die Geschichtstheologie*; however, he does discuss Orosius's general argument that the *tempora Christiana* has brought about milder behavior on the part of barbarians, see esp. pp. 98–99.

25. Orosius, 1.16 p. 65. On Orosius and classical history, see Hervé Inglebert, *Les romains chrétiens face à l'histoire de Rome: Histoire, christianisme et romanités en Occident dans l'Antiquité tardive (IIIe–Ve siècles)* (Paris: Institut d'Etudes Augustiniennes, 1996), pp. 507–92.

26. Orosius, 1.15–16.

27. As Lisa Bitel remarks concerning warrior women as foundational figures, ". . . ultimately they failed at men's wars, or they were domesticated, or both. . . . Either way, they ended up miserable or died young, rendering a double lesson: first, fighting was properly gendered as male so that female fighters, though alluringly heroic were barbarous; and, secondly, the barbarous past was over" (*Women in Early Medieval Europe*, p. 79).

28. Cosmas, *Chronica Boemorum*, book 1. See František Graus, *Lebendige Vergangenheit, Überlieferung im Mittelalter und in den Vorstellungen vom Mittelalter* (Vienna: Böhlau, 1975), pp. 89–106 (on the foundation legends of Bohemia and their transmission and uses in national discourse).

29. Cosmas, 1.3, p. 8.

30. Cosmas, 1.9, pp. 19–20.

31. Cosmas, 1.4, pp. 9–10

32. Cosmas, 1.4, p. 10.

33. Cosmas, 1.4, p. 11.

34. Cosmas, 1.4, p. 11.

35. Cosmas, 1.4, pp. 11–12.

36. Cosmas, 1.4, p. 12.

37. Cosmas, 1.5, p. 14.

38. Cosmas, 1.5, p. 15.

39. In general on Cosmas, see Dušan Třeštík, *Kosmova Kronika: Studie k počátkům českého dějepisectví a politického myšlení* (Prague: Academia, 1968). See also Lisa Wolverton, *Hastening toward Prague: Power and Society in the Medieval Czech Lands* (Philadelphia: University of Pennsylvania Press, 2001).

40. *Chronicon Montis Sereni*, ed. E. Eherenfeuchter, MGH SS 23 (Hanover, 1874), p. 176. Cited by Robert Bartlett in "Reflections on Paganism and Christianity in Medieval Europe," *Proceedings of the British Academy* 101 (1998): 55–76, esp. 61.

41. J. Ludvíkovský ed., *Kristiánova legenda—Legenda Christiani* (Prague: Vyšehrad, 1978), pp. 16–18. On the authenticity of the text and the argument that it dates from ca. 992–94, see Dušan Třeštík, *Počátky Přemyslovců* (Prague: Academia, 1997), pp. 117–36. For an English language summary of the debate, see Marvin Kantor, *The Origins of Christianity in Bohemia: Sources and Commentary* (Evanston, IL: Northwestern University Press, 1990), pp. 18 and 31–46. I am grateful to Professor Dušan Třeštík for his assistance with this text and that of Cosmas.

42. On the construction of Cosmas's text, see Alfred Thomas, *The Labyrinth of the Word: Truth and Representation in Czech Literature* (Munich: R. Oldenbourg, 1995), pp. 33–46, and more generally, Vladimir Karbusický, *Anfänge der historischen Überlieferung in Böhmen: Ein Beitrag zum Vergleichenden Überlieferung in Böhmen*, Ostmitteleuropa in Vergagenheit und Gegenwart 118, (Cologne: Böhlau, 1980). Still fundamental is František Graus, *Lebendige Vergangenheit*, esp. pp. 89–97.

43. Cosmas, 1.4, p. 11.

44. Petri Damiani, *Epistolae*, Lib. 2.13, PL 144:282–83.

45. Cosmas, 1.9, p. 19.

46. Herwig Wolfram, "Ethnographie und die Entstehung neuer ethnischer Identitäten im Frühmittelalter," in Monika Mokre, Gilbert Weiss, and Rainer Bauböck, eds., *Europas Identitäten: Mythen, Konflikte, Konstruktionen* (Frankfurt on the Main: Campus, 2003), pp. 25–35.

47. Cosmas, 1.9, p. 21.

48. The parallels between Libuše and Mathilda have been pointed out by Karbusický, *Anfänge der historischen Überlieferung in Böhmen*, pp. 17–18, although his analysis differs significantly from my own.

49. Cosmas, 2.31, p. 126

50. Cosmas, 2.32, pp. 127–29.

51. "Rerum cunctarum comes indimota mearum, Bis Februi quinis obiit Bozeteha kalendis." Cosmas, 3.43, p. 217.

52. PL 51:611. Cosmas need not have known the poem firsthand. It was quoted by Bede in his *De arte metrica*, PL 90:173 to illustrate Anacreontine meter.

Chapter Three

1. For example, the house of Anjou, which Karl Ferdinand Werner traces to the marriage of Ingelgarius, father of Fulk the Red, and Adelais, a member of the powerful Widonen clan, which launched the fortunes of the family in Brittany and Anjou. Karl Ferdinand Werner, "Untersuchungen zur Frühzeit des französischen Fürstentums (9.–10. Jahrhundert)," *Die Welt als Geschichte* 18 (1958): 264–79. Bernard Bachrach has attempted unconvincingly to refine Werner's research in "Some Observations on the Origins of the Angevin Dynasty," *Medieval Prosopography* 10 (1989): 1–24, which he repeats in *Fulk Nerra, the Neo-Roman Consul, 987–1040: A Political Biography of the Angevin Count* (Berkeley: University of California Press, 1993), pp. 1–4, but see Christian Settipani, "Les comtes d'Anjou et leurs alliances aux Xe et XIe siècles," in K.S.B. Keats-Rohan, ed., *Family Trees and the Roots of Politics: The Prosopography of Britain and France from the Tenth to the Twelfth Century* (Woodbridge, UK: Boydell Press, 1997), pp. 211–69, esp. pp. 212–18. On other such families, see Constance Brittain Bouchard, *Those of My Blood*, esp. pp. 22–38.

2. Anita Guerreau-Jalabert, "Sur les structures de parenté dans l'Europe médiévale," *Annales ESC* 36 (1981), 1028–49; and "La parenté dans l'Europe médiévale et moderne: À propos d'une synthèse recente," *L'Homme* 110 (1989): 69–93.

3. Nelson, "Perceptions du pouvoir chez les historiennes du haute moyen-âge," in *La femme au moyen-âge*, p. 79.

4. The Book of Judith is not part of the Hebrew Bible and thus is counted among the apocrypha. Jerome included it in the Vulgate although the text from which he translated it differs greatly from the Septuagint version.

5. On the ambiguities of Judith in the Anglo-Saxon tradition, see Heide Estes, "Feasting with Holofernes," *Exemplaria* 15 (2003): 325–50. On the conti-

nental receptions of Judith in relationship to the wife of Louis the Pious, see Elizabeth Ward, "Caesar's Wife: The Career of the Empress Judith, 819–829," in Peter Godman and Roger Collins, eds., *Charlemagne's Heir: New Perspectives on the Reign of Louis the Pious (814–840)* (Oxford: Clarendon Press, 1990), pp. 205–27, esp. 222.

6. On the Welfs, see in general Bernd Schneidmüller, *Die Welfen: Herrschaft und Errinerung (819–1252)* (Stuttgart: Verlag W. Kohlhammer, 2000).

7. Karl Schmid, "Welfisches Selbstverständnis," in J. Fleckenstein and Karl Schmid, eds., *Adel und Kirche: Gerd Tellenbach um 65. Geburtstag* (Freiburg: Herder, 1968), pp. 389–416.

8. Especially the studies of Otto Gerhard Oexle, "Die 'sächsische Welfenquelle' als Zeugnis der welfischen Hausüberlieferung," *Deutsches Archiv* 24 (1968): 435–97; Oexle, "Welfische Memoria: Zugleich ein Beitrag über adlige Hausüberlieferung und die Kriterien ihrer Erforschung," in Bernd Schneidmüller, ed., *Die Welfen und ihr Braunschweiger Hof im hohen Mittelalter* (Wiesbaden: Harrossowitz, 1995), pp. 61–94; and among the studies of Bernd Schneidmüller, especially "Landesherrschaft, welfische Indentität und soziale Gruppen im deutschen Mittelalter," in Peter Moraw, ed., *Regionale Identität und soziale Gruppen im deutschen Mittelalter, Zeitschrift für historische Forschung,* Beiheft 14 (Berlin: Duncker and Humblot, 1992), pp. 65–101. However, the extent to which the kin of Welf and his daughter Judith formed a cohesive party in the ninth century can be exaggerated. See Janet L. Nelson, *Charles the Bald* (London: Longman, 1992), pp. 177–80.

9. Thegan, *Gesta Hludowici imperatoris,* ed. Ernst Tremp., MGH SSRG i.u.s. 64 (Hanover, 1995), c. 26, p. 214. See Schmid, "Welfisches Selbstverständnis," n. 12.

10. *Lex Baiwariorum,* 3.1. "De genealogia qui vocantur Hosi, Drazza Fagana Hahilinga Anniona isti sunt quasi primi post Agilolfingos qui sunt de genere ducali," ed. Ernst von Schwind, MGH Leges nationum Germanicarum, sec. 1, vol. 5, part 2 (Hanover, 1926), pp. 312–13. Wolfgang Metz, "Heinrich mit dem goldenen Wagen," in *Blätter für deutsche Landesgeschichte* 107 (1971): 136–61, esp. 148, suggests a connection with the Huosi and other leading Bavarian families. This may be the case, but one should not read the list of Bavarian kindreds as a fixed, exclusive identity. See Karl Brunner, *Oppositionelle Gruppen im Karolingerreich,* Veröffentlichungen des Instituts für österreichische Geschichtsforschung 25 (Vienna: Hermann Böhlaus Nach, 1979), esp. pp. 102–3.

11. Silvia Konecny, "Eherecht und Ehepolitik unter Ludwig dem Frommen," *Mitteilungen des Instituts für österreichische Geschichtsforschung* 85 (1977): 1–21, esp. 15.

12. Bernd Schneidmüller, "Landesherrschaft, welfische Identität und sächsiche Geshichte," in Peter Moraw, ed., *Regionale Identität und soziale Gruppen im deutschen Mittelalter, Zeitschrift für historische Forschung*, Beiheft 14 (Berlin: Duncker and Humblot, 1992), pp. 65–101.

13. Thegan, *Gesta Hludowici imperatoris*, MGH SSRG i.u.s., 64, c. 26, p. 214.

14. *Annales regni Francorum*, ed. Friderich Kurze, MGH SSRG i.u.s. 6 (Hanover, 1895), an. 819, p. 150: "Imperator inspectis plerisque nobilium filiabus Huelpi comitis filiam nomine Iudith duxit uxorem." Astronomus, *Vita Hludowici imperatoris*, ed. Ernst Tremp, MGH SSRG i.u.s. 64 (Hanover, 1995), p. 32. See Brunner, *Oppositionelle Gruppen*, p. 102; Egon Boshof, *Ludwig der Fromme* (Darmstadt: Primus, 1996), p. 152.

15. Hrabanus Maurus, *Epistolae*, no. 17a, ed. Ernst Dümmler, MGH Epistolae 5 (Berlin, 1899), pp. 420–21. See Mayke de Jong, "Bride Shows Revisited: Praise, Slander and Exegesis in the Reign of the Empress Judith," in Leslie Brubaker and Julia M. H. Smith, eds., *Gender in the Early Medieval World*, pp. 257–77.

16. And she paid the price of being branded an adulteress. Geneviève Bührer-Thierry, "La reine adultère," *Cahiers de Civilisation Médiévale* 35 (1992): 299–312. See also Pauline Stafford, *Queens, Concubines, and Dowagers: The King's Wife in the Early Middle Ages* (Athens: University of Georgia Press, 1983), esp. pp. 18–20 and 83; Elizabeth Ward, "Agobard of Lyons and Paschasius Radbertus as Critics of the Empress Judith," in W. J. Sheils and D. Wood, eds., *Women in the Church*, Studies in Church History 27 (Oxford: Blackwell, 1990), pp. 15–25; Ward, "Caesar's Wife"; and de Jong, "Bride Shows Revisited," p. 262.

17. Generally on the Welfs in the later ninth century, see Schneidmüller, *Die Welfen*, pp. 58–72.

18. *Geneologia Welforum*, ed. Georg Pertz, MGH SS 13 (Hanover, 1881), pp. 733–34. See also Oexle, "Welfische Memoria."

19. *Sächsische Weltchronik*, ed. Ludwig Weiland, MGH Deutsche Chroniken 2 (Hanover, 1877), pp. 1–384. See also Oexle, " 'Die sächsische Welfenquelle' "; and Oexle, "Bischof Konrad von Konstanz in der Erinnerung der Welfen und der welfischen Hausüberlieferung während des 12. Jahrhunderts," *Freiburger Diözesan-Archiv* 95 (1975): 7–40; and, for fuller bibliography, Schneidmüller, *Die Welfen*, p. 24 and the literature he cites, n. 10.

20. *Historia Welforum Weingartensis*, ed. Ludwig Weiland, MGH SS 21 (Hanover, 1864), pp. 457–72. Schneidmüller, *Die Welfen*, 24–26.

21. *Geneologia Welforum*, p. 733: "Eticho genuit filium Heinricum et filiam Hiltigardam. Hiltigardam Ludowicus Balbus inperator [*sic*] accepit uxorem.

H[einricus] inperatori hominium facit; pater in Ambergov 12 monachos instituit et ibi obiit. Heinricus monachos Altemunster transtulit, unde eos Wingarten, et dominas inde, que ibi erant, in Altenmunster transposuit. Heinricus Atham duxit uxorem et genuit sanctum Chûnradum Constantiensem episcopum, Ethiconem et Rûdolfum." It continues: "Henry had moved the monks to Altomünster and then to Weingarten and the cannonesses, who had been there, he placed in Altomünster. Henry married Atha and sired Saint Conrad bishop of Constance, Eticho, and Rudolf."

22. "Tempore Pii Lodowici inperatoris, filii Karoli Magni, extitit quidam de principibus Bawarorum, qui fuit binomius, nam et Eticho et Welfus dicebatur; cuius filiam nomine Iudith ipse Lodowicus post mortem Irmingardis inperatricis accepit in coniugium, genuitque ex ea Karolum cesarem Calvum, unde longa filiorum ac nepotum successione claruit regnum Francorum." *Annalista Saxo*, ed. G. Waitz, MGH SS 6, (Hanover, 1844), p. 764.

23. In this regard, one thinks of the account in Dudo of St. Quintin wherein Rollo, when becoming the vassal of King Charles the Simple, refuses to kiss the king's feet as part of the ritual of vassality. He orders one of his men to do it in his place. But this Viking grasps the king's foot and raises it to his lips, thus causing the king to fall over backward—the submission of the duke comes at the cost of the humiliation of the king. Dudo, *De Moribus et actis primorum Normanniae ducum*, PL 141:650–51.

24. *Historia Welforum Weingartensis*, MGH SS 21, pp. 458–59.

25. Gerd Althoff, *Spielregeln der Politik im Mittelalter: Kommunikation in Frieden und Fehde* (Darmstadt: Primus Verlag, 1997).

26. Pauline Stafford, "Charles the Bald, Judith and England," in Margaret T. Gibson and Janet L. Nelson, eds., *Charles the Bald, Court and Kingdom*, 2nd rev. ed. (Aldershot, UK: Variorum, 1990), pp. 139–53. See also Janet L. Nelson's comments in her translation of the *Annals of St-Bertin* (Manchester: Manchester University Press, 1991), p. 83, n. 11.

27. Annals of St.-Bertin, a. 856, MGH: *Annales Bertiniani*, ed. G. Waitz, MGH SSRG i.u.s. 5 (Hanover, 1883), an. 856, p. 47. Nelson, *Annals of St.-Bertin*, pp. 81–83.

28. Nelson, trans., *Annals of St.-Bertin*, an. 862, p. 97.

29. For example, Jean Dunbabin, *France in the Making, 843–1180* (Oxford: Oxford University Press, 1980), p. 69.

30. "Balduinum comitem, ipso lenocinante, et fratre suo Hludowico consentiente, mutato habitu est secuta." *Annales Bertiniani*, MGH SSRG i.u.s. 5, pp. 56–57. Nelson, trans., *Annales of St.-Bertin*, p. 97. See also her remarks in Nelson, *Charles the Bald* (London: Longman, 1992), p. 203.

31. David Nicholas, *Medieval Flanders* (London: Longman, 1992), p. 17.

32. Nicholas, *Medieval Flanders*, pp. 17–18; Rosamond McKitterick, *The Frankish Kingdoms under the Carolingians, 751–987* (London: Longman, 1983), pp. 248–50.

33. Witger, *Genealogia Arnulfi Comitis*, ed. L. C. Bethmann, MGH SS 9, (Hanover, 1851), pp. 302–4.

34. On the relationship between the Carolingian genealogy and St. Bertin, see Helmut Reimitz, "Anleitung zur Interpretation: Schrift und Genealogie in der Karolingerzeit," in Walter Pohl and Paul Herold, eds., *Vom Nutzen des Schreibens*, Forschungen zur Geschichte des Mittelalters 5 (Vienna: Verlag der Österreichischen Akademie der Wissenschaften, 2002), pp. 167–82, and esp. n. 45. Compare the *Commemoratio genealogiae domni Karoli* to the Flemish genealogy.

35. Witger, *Genealogia*, p. 303, "HIC INCIPIT SANCTA PROSAPIA DOMNI AR-NULFI COMITIS GLORIOSSISSIMI FILIQUE EIUS BALDUINI QUOS DOMINUS IN HOC SECULO DIGNETUR PROTOGERE."

36. "Quam Iudith prudentissimam ac spetiosam sociavit sibi Balduinus comes fortissimos in matrimonii conjugium. Ex qua genuit filium, inponens ei nomen sibi equivocum, videlicet Balduinum." Ibid., p. 303.

37. On the importance of the Carolingian origin of the family to Witger, see Gert Melville, "Vorfahren und Vorgänger: Spätmittelalterliche Genealogien als dynastische Legitimation zur Herrschaft," in Peter-Johannes Schuler, ed., *Die Familie als sozialer und historischer Verband: Untersuchungen zum Spätmittelalter und zur frühen Neuzeit* (Sigmaringen: Jan Thorbecke Verlag, 1987), pp. 203–309, esp. 267–69 and the literature there cited.

38. "Lidricus Harlebeccensis comes genuit Ingelrannum. Ingelrannus genuit Audacrum. Audacer genuit Balduinum Ferreum, qui duxit filiam Karoli Calvi nomine Judith." *Geneaologia comitum Flandriae Bertiana*, MGH SS 9, p. 305.

39. "Balduinus Ferreus genuit Balduinum Calvum, qui duxit filiam Edgeri regis Anglorum, nominee Elftruden." Ibid.

40. "Balduinus autem Ferreus genuit Balduinum Calvum ex Judith vidua Adelbaldi Regis Anglorum, filia videlicet Karoli Calvi regis Francorum. Hic prius eam duxerat, et anno eodem quo eam accepit, obit. Quo defuncto, Judith, possessionibus venditis, quas in Anglorum regno obtinuerat, ad patrem rediit, et Silvanectis, Sentliz sub tuitione paterna servabatur." Lambert, *Genealogia comitum Flandriae*, MGH SS 9, p. 309.

41. "Anno igitur dominicae incarnationis 862 Balduinus Ferreus rapuit Judith, viduam Adelbaldi regis Anglorum et filiam Karoli Calvi regis Francorum . . ." MGH SS 9, p. 317.

42. "... Iudith, qui comitem propter probitatem suam valde diligebat ..." "Nicholaus autem videns eum iuventem pulcherrimum et probum ..." Ibid.

43. See Karen S. Nicholas, "Countesses as Rulers in Flanders," in Theodore Evergates, ed., *Aristocratic Women in Medieval France*, pp. 111–37.

CHAPTER FOUR

1. Without attempting to do justice to the vast literature on the cult of Mary, one can begin with Jaroslav Pelikan, *Mary through the Centuries: Her Place in the History of Culture* (New Haven, CT: Yale University Press, 1996). On historical approaches to the cult of Mary in the Middle Ages, see Hedwig Röckelein et al., *Maria Abbild oder Vorbild?*

2. In particular, see Carolyn C. Wilson, *St. Joseph in Italian Renaissance Society and Art: New Directions and Interpretations* (Philadelphia: Saint Joseph's University Press, 2001), esp. pp. 3–11; and Sheila Schwartz, "Symbolic Allusions in a Twelfth-Century Ivory," *Marsyas* 16 (1972–73): 35–42. While these scholars convincingly argue for a more positive tradition concerning Joseph prior to the Reformation, the fact remains that Joseph was, in spite of a series of attempts by theologians and preachers to develop his cult, marginal to Western medieval religion and at times clearly denigrated.

3. Wilson, *St. Joseph*, pp. 3–4.

4. See generally Anita Guerreau-Jalabert, "L'Arbre de Jessé et l'ordre chrétien de la parenté," in Dominique Iogna-Prat, Éric Palazzo, and Daniel Russo, eds., *Marie: Le culte de la vierge dans la société médiévale* (Paris: Beauchesne, 1996), pp. 137–70. On the development of the cult of Mary's nativity and the image of the Jesse tree, see Margot Fassler, "Mary's Nativity, Fulbert of Chartres, and the *Stirps Jesse*: Liturgical Innovation circa 1000 and Its Afterlife," *Speculum* 75 (2000): 389–434, esp. 390–91 on the development of the image of the Jesse Tree.

5. With the exception of the bronze doors of San Zeno in Verona, the Virgin is always present, a constant that has led some to describe the Tree of Jesse as a genealogy of the Virgin, a characterization denied by Anita Guerreau-Jalabert, "L'Arbre de Jessé," p. 163.

6. Pierpont Morgan Library, New York, M.724v. I am grateful to Elizabeth Parker McLachlan for bringing this image to my attention and for sharing with me her unpublished essay, "The Jesse Tree of Morgan 724v and Early Sources for the Canterbury Picture Leaves."

7. Guerreau-Jalabert, "L'Arbre de Jessé":"La Vierge occupe dans le dispositif iconographique une position-clé, puisqu'elle correspond précisément

au pivot, à la charnière autour de laquelle s'opère le passage d'une forme de parenté à l'autre" (p. 162).

8. *Biblia Latina cum glossa ordinaria*, 4.6.

9. For a comprehensive guide to the enormous literature on the genealogical materials in the Gospels and related issues, see Raymond Edward Brown, *The Birth of the Messiah: A Commentary on the Infancy Narratives in Matthew and Luke* (Garden City, NY: Doubleday, 1977).

10. Ruperti Abbatis Tuitiensis, *De gloria et honore Filii hominis Super Matthaeum*, 1, PL 168:1317.

11. M. Yeboamot, 4:13. *The Mishnah, Seder Nashim*, vol. 1 of *Yevamot: A New Translation with a Commentary by Rabbi Pinhas* Kehati, trans. Edward Levin, ed. Rabbi Bernard Susser (Jerusalem: Eliner Library Department for Torah Education and Culture in the Diaspora of the World Zionist Organization, 1992), p. 72.

12. Origen, *Contra Celsum*, trans. with an introduction and notes by Henry Chadwick (Cambridge: Cambridge University Press, 1980), 1.32, p. 31.

13. The Gospel of Nicodemus: Acts of Pilate and Christ's Descent into Hell," in Edgar Hennecke, *Neutestamentliche Apokryphen*, ed. Wilhelm Schneemelcher. English Translation by A.J.B. Higgins et al., *New Testament Apocrypha*, ed. R. McL. Wilson, vol. 1, *Gospels and Related Writings* (Philadelphia: Westminster Press, 1963), pp. 444–83.

14. 3 "Then the elders of the Jews answered and said to Jesus: 'What should we see? Firstly, that you were born of fornication; secondly, that your birth meant the death of the children in Bethlehem; thirdly, that you father Joseph and your mother Mary fled into Egypt because they counted for nothing among the people. Then declared some of the Jews that stood by, devout men: 'We deny that he came of fornication, for we know that Joseph was betrothed to Mary, and he was not born of fornication.' Pilate then said to the Jews who said that he came of fornication: 'Your statement is not true; for there was a betrothal, as your own fellow-countrymen say.' Annas and Caiaphas say to Pilate: 'We, the whole multitude, cry out that he was born of fornication, and we are not believed; there are proselytes and disciples of his." And Pilate called to him Annas and Caiaphas and said to them: 'What are proselytes?' They answered: 'They were born children of Greeks, and now have become Jews.' Then said those who said that he was not born of fornication, namely Lazarus, Asterius, Antonius, Jacob, Amnes, Zeras, Samuel, Isaac, Phineës, Crispus, Agrippa, and Judas: 'We are not proselytes, but are children of Jews and speak the truth; for we were present at the betrothal of Joseph and Mary.' " Ibid., pp. 453–54.

15. Eusebius, *History of the Church*, 3.11 and 4.22, trans. G. A. Williamson (Baltimore: Penguin Books, 1965), pp. 123–24 and 181–82. The relationship is even more complicated by the statement in John that Clopas's wife Mary was the sister of the mother of Jesus. This would suggest that the two brothers married two sisters, Mariam and Maria.

16. P. Vogt, *Der Stammbaum Christi bei den heiligen Evangelisten Matthäus* (Freiburg: Herder, 1907), pp. 15–16.

17. Eusebius, *History of the Church*, 3.18–20, pp. 125–27. See Brown, *The Birth of the Messiah*, appendix 2, "Davidic Descent," pp. 505–12, esp. 506.

18. In general on the infancy narratives in Matthew and Luke, see Brown, *Birth of the Messiah*.

19. Current scholarly consensus argues that this reading is the preferred. However, other readings are less explicit about denying that Joseph was the father of Jesus, including "Jacob was the Father of Joseph, to whom the betrothed virgin Mary bore Jesus, called the Christ"; and, in the Old Syriac Sinaiticus version: "Joseph, to whom the virgin Mary was betrothed, was the father of Jesus, called the Christ." See Brown, *Birth of the Messiah*, pp. 62–63.

20. Eusebius, *History of the Church*, 1.7, pp. 53–54.

21. Deut. 25:5–6.

22. Eusebius, *History of the Church*, 1.7, pp. 53–54.

23. Ibid. Actually, Eusebius is in error, since marriage within towns and clans is not mentioned in Mosaic law nor does marriage within tribes concern anyone but heiresses. For problems with the levirate marriage hypothesis, see Brown, *Birth of the Messiah*, app. 1, "Levirate Marriage," pp. 503–4.

24. The Julius Africanus solution was popular both in the Greek and Latin churches. See, for example, the Greek genealogy edited by François Halkin, "Une généalogie de Saint Joseph," *Analecta Bollandiana* 87 (1969): 372.

25. Oscar Cullmann, trans., "The Protoevangelium of James," in *Gospels and Related Writings*, vol. 1 of *New Testament Apocrypha*, pp. 370–88. See also Kathleen Ashley and Pamela Sheingorn, eds., *Interpreting Cultural Symbols: Saint Anne in Late Medieval Society* (Athens: University of Georgia Press, 1990), pp. 6–10.

26. Jerome, *De virginitate B. Mariae*, PL 23:183–206.

27. This treatise was identified by Paul Monceaux as that contained in Manuscript T used by Theodor Mommsen in his edition, which he terms, after the title carried by later, African versions, the *Liber genealogus*. MGH AA 9, pp. 154–96. See Paul Monceaux, *Histoire littéraire de l'Afrique chrétienne depuis les origines jusqu'à l'invasion arabe* VI: *Littérature donatiste au temps de Saint Augustin* (Paris: Editions Ernest Leroux, 1922), esp. p. 253. See also Christiane Klapisch-Zuber, *L'ombre des ancêtres: Essai sur l'imaginaire médiéval de la*

parenté. (Paris: Fayard, 2000), pp. 65–67. On the manuscript tradition, see Richard Rouse and Charles McNelis, "North African Literary Activity: A Cyprian Fragment, the Stichometric Lists and a Donatist Compendium," *Revue d'histoire des Textes* 30 (2000): 189–238, esp. 219–24.

28. "Iacob genuit Ioseph id est congregans, cuius ut putabatur dominus christus secundum carnem esse filius." *Liber genealogus,* MGH AA 9, p. 185.

29. "Ioseph genuit Ioachim. [An alternative version adds "Iachim genuit matrem Mariam matrem domini iesu Christi."] Hanc progeniem secundum Nathan introducit Lucas et secundum Salamonem Mattheus, ut cognoscatur ex una radice Iesse, id est David venire Ioseph sive Maria mater." *Liber genealogus,* MGH AA 9, p. 194.

30. On the genealogies in the Beatus manuscripts, see Yolanta Załuska, "Les feuillets liminaires," in *El "Beato" de Saint-Sever: Ms. Lat. 8878 de la Bibliothèque nationale de Paris* (Madrid: Edilán, 1984), pp. 239–54, esp. 241–44.

31. John of Damascus, *De fide orthodoxa: Versions of Burgundio and Cerbanus,* ed. Eligius M. Buytaert (St. Bonaventure, NY: Franciscan Institute, 1955), ch. 87.5, p. 320.

32. Jacobus de Voragine, *The Golden Legend Readings on the Saints,* trans. William Granger Ryan, 2 vols. (Princeton, NJ: Princeton University Press, 1993), 2:149–58.

33. Jerome, *De perpetua virginitate B. Mariae Liber,* 13, PL 23:196.

34. See J. K. Elliott, *The Apocryphal New Testament: A Collection of Apocryphal Christian Literature in an English Translation* (Oxford: Clarendon Press, 1993), pp. 85–99. See also Fassler, "Mary's Nativity," esp. pp. 397–99.

35. Haymo Halberstatensis [*sic*] episcopi, *Historiae sacrae epitome* 2.3, PL 118:823–24. See also Ashley and Sheingorn, *Interpreting Cultural Symbols,* pp. 10–11. On the identity of the Haymo, see Baudouin de Gaiffier, "Le Trinubium Annae," *Analecta Bollandiana* 90 (1972): 289–98.

36. On the iconography of Joseph and Mary on the flight into Egypt, see Lucette Valensi, *La fuite en Égypte: Histoires d'Orient et d'Occident* (Paris: Seuil, 2002); and Sheila Schwartz, "St. Joseph in Meister Bertram's Petri-Altar," *Gesta* 24, no. 2 (1985): 147–56.

37. Paolo Testini, "Alle origini dell'iconografia di Giuseppe de Nazareth," *Rivista di Archeologia Cristiana* 48 (1972): 271–347. But see Pamela Sheingorn, " 'Illustris partiarcha Joseph': Jean Gerson, Representations of Saint Joseph, and Imagining Community among Churchmen in the Fifteenth Century," in Nicholas Howe, ed., *Visions of Community in the Pre-Modern World* (Notre Dame, IN: University of Notre Dame Press, 2002), pp. 75–108.

38. See Wilson, *St. Joseph,* pp. 3–9 for the most that one can deduce concerning such a cult. See Sheingorn, " 'Illustris partiarcha Joseph' " on the limits of such attempts.

39. Wilson, *St. Joseph*, p. 11, identifies the earliest known church dedication to St. Joseph as San Giuseppe di Borgo Galliera in Bologna, which dates from the twelfth century. One church does not a popular cult make.

40. See Sheingorn, "Illustris partiarcha Joseph,' " on the failure of Gerson's efforts.

41. Sheila Schwartz, in "St. Joseph in Meister Bertram's Petri-Altar," p. 154, n. 21 and pp. 155–56 n. 33, argues that the interpretation of ridicule in such representations is an error.

EPILOGUE

1. Paulus Diaconus, 1.15.

Suggestions for Further Reading

A rich and growing literature in English, but also especially in German and in French, is renewing how we understand the strategies that wrote women into and out of ancient and medieval texts while exploring through this literature the complicated worlds in which real women lived. For a better understanding of women in classical literature and society, one should consult Elaine Fantham, et al., *Women in the Classical World: Image and Text* (New York: Oxford University Press, 1994); Nicole Loraux, *Les enfants d'Athéna: Idées athéniennes sur la citoyenneté et la division des sexes* (Paris: François Maspero, 1981); Melissa M. Matthes, *The Rape of Lucretia and the Founding of Republics: Readings in Livy, Machiavelli and Rousseau* (University Park: Pennsylvania State University Press, 2000); Marie Theres Fögen, *Römische Rechtsgeschichten: Über Ursprung und Evolution eines sozialen Systems* (Göttingen: Vandenhoeck and Ruprecht, 2002); Jean-Claude Schmitt, ed., *Ève et Pandora: La création de la femme* (Paris: Gallimard, 2001); and Robert Rollinger and Christoph Ulf, eds., *Geschlechterrollen und Frauenbild in der Perspektive antiker Autoren* (Innsbruck: Studien Verlag, 2000).

A similar rich literature is developing a new and nuanced understanding of the representation of women in medieval literature, among them Lisa M. Bitel, *Women in Early Medieval Europe, 400–1100* (Cambridge: Cambridge University Press, 2002); Leslie Brubaker and Julia M. H. Smith, eds., *Gender in the Early Medieval World: East and West, 300–900* (Cambridge: Cambridge University Press, 2004); Mary C. Erler and Maryanne Kowaleski, eds., *Gendering the Master Narrative: Women and Power in the Middle Ages* (Ithaca, NY: Cornell University Press, 2003); Constance Brittain Bouchard, *Those of My Blood: Constructing Noble Families in Medieval Francia* (Philadelphia: University of Pennsylvania Press, 2001); Theodore Evergates, ed., *Aristocratic Women in Medieval France* (Philadelphia: University of Pennsylvania Press, 1999); and Christiane Klapisch-Zuber, *L'ombre des ancêstres: Essai sur l'imaginaire médiéval de la parenté* (Paris: Fayard, 2000).

Particularly important are studies of Mary and Anna as models or exemplars: Kathleen Ashley and Pamela Sheingorn, eds., *Interpreting Cultural Symbols:*

Saint Anne in Late Medieval Society (Athens: University of Georgia Press, 1990); Lucette Valensi, *La fuite en Égypte: Histoires d'Orient et d'Occident* (Paris: Seuil, 2002); Hedwig Röckelein, Claudia Opitz, and Dieter R. Bauer, eds., *Maria Abbild oder Vorbild? Zur Sozialgeschichte mittelalterlicher Marienverehrung* (Tübingen: Edition Diskord, 1990); and Dominique Iogna-Prat, Éric Palazzo, and Daniel Russo, eds., *Marie: Le culte de la vierge dans la société médiévale* (Paris: Beauchesne, 1996).

Index

"Acts of Pilate," 65
Adaloald, 23
Adam (biblical), 16–17
Adam of Bremen, 27
Adelbald, 52
Adelheid, 46
Aelfthryth, 54–55
Aeneas, 15
Aeneid (Virgil), 15
Æthelbald, 52
Æthelwulf, 52
Africanus, Julius, 67–68
Agathyrsus, 13
Agelmund, 24
Agilulf, 23
Aigo, 23
Alboin, 3
Alexander legends, 27
Alfred the Great, 54–55
Alpheo, 72
Althoff, Gerd, 51
Amalberga, 3
Amazons, 8–9, 26–42; archaeological
    evidence of, 9, 28; Czechs and, 9, 34–
    42; Goths and, 26–34, 76; Lombards
    and, 27
Ambrose, Saint, 11
Anglo-Saxon Chronicle, 21
Anglo-Saxons, 21–22
Anna, 69–70, 72, 74, 77
Annales regni Francorum, 46
Annals of St. Bertin, 52–53, 55–57
Appius Claudius, 16
Arioald, 23
Arnulf I, 54–55
Arpoxaïs, 12
Astronomer, the, 46
Athena, 14

Athenian traditions, 14–15
Aurelian, 30–32
Authari, 23

Babel, tower of, 17
Bachrach, Bernard, 88n1
Baldwin I (Baldwin Iron Arm), 53–57, 59
Baldwin II, 54–55
Baldwin III, 54
Baswell, Christopher, 15
Beatus commentaries, 71, 74
Bede, 21, 27
Bernard of Clairvaux, 62, 73
Bitel, Lisa, 24, 86n27
Bloch, Marc, 7–10
Bloch, R. Howard, 11
Bohemians. *See* Czechs
Bouchard, Constance, 43
Burgundo of Pisa, 71

Carthage (city), 15
Celsus, 65
Charlemagne, 51, 57
Charles the Bald, 46–47, 49, 52–54
Chronicle of Fredegar, 27
classical traditions, 4, 9, 11–16, 27
Clementia of Burgundy, 58
Cleopha, 72
Cleph, 23
Clopas, 66, 71
Clothild, 3
Clovis, 3
Colaxaïs, 12
Contra Celsum (Origen), 65
Cosmas of Prague, 3, 9, 19, 27, 29, 34–35,
    37–38, 40–42, 76
Council of Ephesus, 73
Crocco, 35
Czechs, 3, 9, 34–42

DATE DUE

APR 2 5 2012		